For

Those Who Design Dreams

And Sell with Heart

Publisher : notionpress.com

Notion Press, Inc.
800, West EL Camino Real #180,
California USA 94040

Notion Press Media Pvt Ltd,
#7, Red Cross Road,
Egmore, Chennai, Tamil Nadu 600008

Title :
The Interior Designer's Sales Blueprint
Mastering Sales for Interior Designers

First Addition : 2025
Published in India
ISBN : Mentioned at back cover page
Author : Gopal Dwivedi
Infographics : Gopal Dwivedi

THE INTERIOR DESIGNER'S SALES BLUEPRINT

Mastering Sales for Interior Designers

GOPAL DWIVEDI

Foreword

As designers, we thrive on creativity, shaping dreams into tangible realities. However, in our immersion in the artistic process, we often overlook the crucial aspects of sales, marketing, and business management. Every design business is a delicate balance between creativity and commercial success—yet, mastering this balance is rarely a part of our formal training.

Gopal Dwivedi, with over 25 years of experience in the interior design industry as an educator, product developer, and business builder, has filled this gap with a definitive guide to selling and sustaining a design business. His book provides creatives with not just insights but also actionable tools to navigate the business side of design effectively.

Despite running my own design firm for 19 years, I found myself missing out on key aspects like 'scope change forms'—a simple yet powerful tool that could have saved me significant time and money. This book sheds light on such overlooked essentials, from client handling and follow-ups to budgeting and systematic project management. Whether you are a beginner or a seasoned professional, this book will undoubtedly offer you valuable takeaways. Thank you, Gopal, for this much-needed resource. Wishing you the very best!

Arch. Priyanka Arjun
Priyanka Arjun and Associates

Acknowledgement

Writing this book has been a deeply fulfilling journey. First and foremost, I extend my heartfelt gratitude to my family—my mother, **Jaya,** whose unwavering belief in me has been my strength; my wife, **Priyanka's** journey has been a key inspiration for this book. I watched her evolve from an interior designer to a sales expert, overcoming challenges and mastering the art of selling design. Her growth made me realize that many designers struggle not due to a lack of talent, but due to a lack of guidance. This book aims to bridge that gap, helping others learn sales more efficiently, and my two wonderful daughters, **Hiya** and **Myra**, whose smiles remind me every day of the importance of balance, passion, and purpose.

I also wish to acknowledge the incredible interior design community that has enriched my journey over the past 21 years. To my colleagues, mentors, and peers at **Livspace.com**, whose dedication to transforming homes has been a constant source of motivation—thank you. This book is dedicated to every designer striving to master the business of design, to sell with confidence, and to turn their creativity into success. Your passion fuels this industry, and I hope this book serves as a valuable companion in your journey.

With heartfelt gratitude
Gopal Dwivedi

Preface

Interior design is more than just creating beautiful spaces—it's about understanding people, their lifestyles, and their unique needs. While creativity and technical skills are fundamental, an often-overlooked aspect of success in this field is the ability to sell design concepts effectively. Many talented designers struggle not because of a lack of expertise but because they find it difficult to communicate their value, handle client objections, and close deals with confidence. This book was born out of a need to bridge that gap. It provides interior designers with a structured approach to sales, offering practical strategies for client engagement, lead generation, negotiation, and closing projects successfully.

Whether you are an independent designer or part of a larger firm, the ability to sell your ideas is essential in a competitive industry. By mastering sales techniques tailored specifically for interior designers, you can elevate your business, build stronger client relationships, and ensure long-term success. This book is not about aggressive sales tactics but about positioning yourself as a trusted consultant, guiding clients toward the best design decisions while maintaining your creative integrity and financial profitability. Let this book be your blueprint for turning design talent into a thriving business

INDEX : 1

INDEX : 2

INDEX : 3

INDEX : 4

Introduction

Introduction

In today's competitive world of residential interior design, **technical expertise alone is no longer enough**. To thrive in this industry, interior designers must evolve beyond just creating beautiful spaces; they must also master the art of selling their ideas, building trust with clients, and delivering solutions that balance **budget, space, and client vision**. This book is designed to bridge that gap, offering a **practical guide** to help interior designers—whether new to the industry or seasoned professionals, to develop the essential skills required to succeed in the business of design.

Why Sales Skills Matter for Interior Designers?

Interior design is a deeply **client-centered profession**, and the most successful designers are not just talented creatives—they are effective communicators, consultants, and project managers. Yet many interior designers struggle with the sales process, often feeling uncomfortable or unsure when it comes to turning initial leads into loyal clients. This book addresses those challenges head-on.

As renowned designer **Kelly Wearstler** once said, *"Interior design is about more than just aesthetics; it's about understanding the lives of the people you're designing for."* To do this well, designers must engage with their clients on a deeper level, learning to ask the right questions, identify underlying needs, and create solutions that exceed expectations. This book will guide you through that process, giving you the tools to develop strong, lasting relationships with clients, while also ensuring your projects stay on time, on budget, and in line with the client's desires.

In the words of **John Saladino**, a celebrated figure in international design, "A room should never allow the eye to settle in one place. It should smile at you and create fantasy." But to deliver such a space, the designer must first sell the vision. **Ramakant Sharma,** founder of Livspace echoes this sentiment, saying that "a combination of good design and a designer who can sell it is rare and precious." He believes that a designer's ability to connect their vision to the client's dream is what brings spaces to life. "When the designer can both envision and articulate that dream, the result is a living experience, not just a space."

This book teaches you how to convey your design ideas in a way that not only resonates with your clients but also aligns with their practical and financial realities.

What you will learn?

This book is a comprehensive guide designed to help you navigate the **client relationship lifecycle** in interior design, from the moment you first meet a potential client to the successful handover of the finished space.

You'll learn **how to engage clients, identify their true needs, offer tailored solutions**, and execute projects that satisfy both the emotional and functional aspects of interior design.

In this book, you will explore:

1. **Client Persona Mapping** – Understand the different types of residential clients, their motivations, and their specific needs. You'll learn how to tailor your approach to each client type, ensuring that your designs resonate deeply with their lifestyle and aspirations.

2. **Client Need Analysis** – Develop the skills to ask the right questions, uncover hidden desires, and interpret client feedback effectively. You'll learn techniques to balance client expectations with the realities of space constraints and budget limits.

3. **Solution Selling** – Go beyond just offering design ideas—learn to sell complete solutions. You'll be taught how to present concepts, manage objections, and demonstrate the value of your design work in a way that convinces clients to invest in your services.

4. **Building Trust and Rapport** – Trust is at the heart of every successful client-designer relationship. This book will provide you with strategies for establishing yourself as a trusted consultant, ensuring long-term client loyalty and repeat business.

5. **Managing Projects and Expectations** – Once you've sold your design vision, the real work begins. This book guides you through the project management process, teaching you how to manage timelines, budgets, and client communications effectively. You'll learn how to avoid common pitfalls that lead to dissatisfaction and missed deadlines.

6. **Embedded Tools and Formats** – This book is equipped with a range of practical tools and formats designed to streamline the design-to-delivery process. These resources will help you organize each stage of your project effectively, ensuring a seamless and professional client experience.

Why this book is essential for your success?

Interior designers often excel at the creative side of the job, but many find themselves overwhelmed when it comes to the **business aspects**—such as client acquisition, project management, and sales. According to industry experts, the ability to **articulate your value** as a designer is one of the most critical skills you can develop.

A 2022 report by **Houzz** found that 60% of clients choose a designer based on their ability to communicate and deliver a solution that fits their needs, not just on the designer's portfolio of work.

This book offers a **step-by-step framework** for integrating effective sales techniques into your design practice, enabling you to confidently take on clients, offer creative solutions, and run your projects smoothly from start to finish. In doing so, you'll be following in the footsteps of some of the world's most successful designers, who know that **selling ideas is just as important as creating them**.

Whether you're an independent designer building your business or working within a firm, mastering these sales skills will set you apart from your competitors and help you build a thriving career.

Peter Marino, an acclaimed architect and interior designer, emphasizes, *"The goal is to create spaces that reflect not just the designer's vision but the client's soul."*

This book will help you discover how to align your designs with your client's deepest desires, ensuring both you and your client are satisfied with the results.

By the end of this book, you will not only be a better designer but also a more confident, effective salesperson, equipped with the knowledge and tools to **succeed in the competitive world of residential interior design**.

1.

Setting the Foundation

1.1 The Role of Sales in Interior Design

1.2 Challenges Without a Defined Sales Process

1.3 Building Trust and Client Relationships

1.4 Designers as Consultants and Problem Solvers

Scan here
for more
digital
content

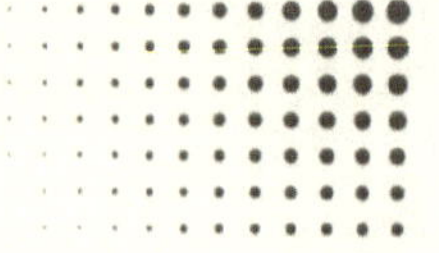

1.0

Setting the Foundation

Executive Summary

In interior design, sales skills are as critical as creativity and technical expertise. This chapter highlights that effective communication, trust-building, and expectation management are essential for turning prospects into loyal clients and ensuring project success. While many designers focus on honing their artistic abilities, mastering sales enables them to communicate value, establish trust, and stand out in a competitive market.

A structured sales process allows designers to avoid common pitfalls such as struggling to close deals, managing scope creep, and dealing with unclear budgets. By positioning themselves as consultants, designers can attract high-quality clients and foster long-term relationships.

Building trust is essential to successful client-designer relationships. From the first consultation, designers should communicate clearly, set realistic expectations, and demonstrate professionalism. This client-centered approach creates a reliable experience that reassures clients and builds lasting partnerships.

Today's designers are both artists and problem-solvers, needing a consultative approach to turn client visions into practical, beautiful solutions. This chapter lays the groundwork for developing these skills, positioning designers for consistent project success and client satisfaction.

1.1

The Role of Sales in Interior Design

While many interior designers focus on honing their creative and technical abilities, **sales skills** are often overlooked. However, these skills are fundamental to success, especially in a field where designers must work closely with clients to interpret their vision and translate it into reality. Here's why sales are essential:

- **Client-Designer Relationship**: Interior designers often work on projects that require significant financial and emotional investment from clients. Without the ability to communicate value effectively, even the most skilled designers may struggle to turn leads into signed contracts.

- **Trust and Confidence**: Clients are entrusting their homes, offices, or personal spaces to you, which means they need to feel confident that you understand their needs and can deliver. **Selling** your ability to meet those needs is just as important as the design itself.

- **Differentiating Your Services**: In a competitive market, sales skills help you distinguish yourself from other designers. By positioning yourself as a **consultant** who provides tailored solutions, you can attract high-quality clients and long-term business relationships.

Key Point: Sales skills are not about being "pushy" but about **communicating value** in a way that resonates with clients' needs and helps them feel confident in your ability to deliver the best design solution.

1.2

Challenges Without a Defined Sales Process

Many designers, especially those just starting in the industry, find themselves facing several challenges due to a lack of structured sales processes. Here are some of the common issues:

- **Difficulty Closing Deals**: Designers without a clear sales strategy often struggle to convert leads into paying clients. This is usually due to a lack of confidence in how to present proposals, handle objections, and close deals effectively.

- **Unclear Client Expectations**: Without a strong focus on understanding and managing client expectations early in the process, designers can end up with dissatisfied clients who feel their vision wasn't fully captured.

- **Scope Creep and Budget Overruns**: Failing to establish clear agreements and expectations around project scope and budget from the outset can lead to **scope creep**, where clients request more work than initially agreed upon, and project overruns, resulting in financial strain.

- **Trust Issues**: Clients often enter the design process with uncertainty, especially when it involves a large financial investment. Designers who can't clearly articulate their value and process may struggle to build the necessary trust to guide the client through the project successfully.

Key Point: Designers without a sales strategy may struggle to maintain control over projects, communicate effectively with clients, and build long-term client relationships. Developing a structured sales process helps to avoid these pitfalls and ensure smoother project execution.

1.3

Building Trust and Client Relationships

Trust is the foundation of every successful client-designer relationship. Clients are not just purchasing a design service; they are **entrusting you** with their vision for an important space in their lives—whether it's a home, office, or commercial space. To build trust, designers must excel in both their craft and their communication.

- **First Impressions Matter**: The initial consultation is a critical moment to establish trust. This is when the designer should demonstrate professionalism, expertise, and a genuine interest in understanding the client's needs.

- **Clear Communication**: Designers must learn how to communicate their ideas in a way that makes clients feel comfortable and confident in the process.This involves listening carefully to the client's desires, explaining design choices clearly, and providing regular updates throughout the project.

- **Transparency**: Being upfront about potential challenges, timelines, and costs is crucial. Clients appreciate honesty, and addressing possible issues head-on fosters trust. Clear communication about **pricing, timelines, and potential project challenges** can alleviate misunderstandings later.

- **Consistency**: Follow-through is just as important as the initial consultation. Consistent communication, meeting deadlines, and delivering on promises helps maintain trust throughout the project.

Key Point: Building a long-lasting client relationship is about being dependable, transparent, and proactive. Clients need to feel that their project is in capable hands, and a strong sales process ensures that trust is built and maintained from the start.

1.4

Designers as Consultants and Problem Solvers

Today's interior designers are more than just **creators of beautiful spaces**, they are **consultants and problem solvers**. Clients often come to designers with vague ideas or conflicting needs. It's the designer's job to help clarify those ideas and turn them into a cohesive, functional, and aesthetically pleasing solution.

- **Consultative Approach**: Great interior designers don't just present readymade ideas; they **collaborate with clients** to discover their needs and create custom solutions. This means listening to concerns, asking the right questions, and helping clients understand the balance between their vision, budget, and the available space.

- **Problem-Solving Mindset**: Every project presents challenges—whether it's working within budget constraints, dealing with awkward layouts, or managing tight deadlines. The ability to **problem-solve creatively** sets successful designers apart. This not only requires design expertise but also a client-centered sales approach that reassures clients throughout the process.

- **Managing Expectations**: Often, clients come with a grand vision that might not align with their budget or the realities of the space. The designer's role is to **guide clients** through the decision-making process, helping them make choices that satisfy both their desires and their practical needs.

This is where the designer shifts from simply offering design solutions to **consulting on the best way forward**.

Key Point: Interior designers must adopt a consultative mindset, guiding clients through the design process while solving problems and managing expectations. This requires a blend of creativity, communication, and sales skills, as designers must not only deliver a design but also ensure it aligns with client needs, budget, and space limitations.

Conclusion

Sales skills are not an optional extra for interior designers—they are fundamental to building a successful practice. By mastering the art of **building trust, understanding client needs, and effectively communicating value**, designers can differentiate themselves in a competitive market. With a solid sales process in place, interior designers can ensure that every project starts on the right foot and ends with a satisfied client and a beautifully executed design.

This book will guide you through the key steps of **sales mastery** in interior design, empowering you to **secure more clients**, **manage expectations**, and **deliver outstanding projects** that result in long-term relationships and repeat business.

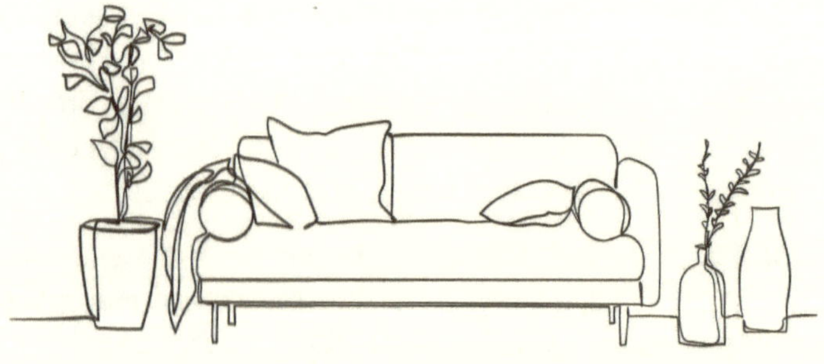

2.

Generating & Qualifying Leads

2.1 Ways to Attract the Right Clients

2.2 The Right Questions to Qualify Leads

2.3 High-Value Leads vs. Low-Priority Inquiries

2.4 Best Ways to Approach Leads

2.5 Scheduling the First Consultation

2.6 Identifying Red Flags in Leads

Tools & Formats:

2.7 Lead Capture Forms

2.8 Lead Qualification Checklist

Scan here
for more
digital
content

2.0

Generating & Qualifying Leads

Executive Summary

In the highly competitive field of residential interior design, generating and qualifying leads is essential to building a steady pipeline of potential clients. Unlike many other industries, interior design involves personal and emotional decision-making for clients, which means that the lead generation process must go beyond just attracting inquiries. It involves capturing the right kind of client, qualifying their needs, and ensuring that they are a good fit for your services.

The Indian market for interior design has seen significant growth in recent years, with estimates suggesting that the interior design industry in India is valued at around INR 20,000 crore, and is expected to grow at a compound annual growth rate (CAGR) of 7% by 2027 . This growth offers opportunities for designers, but it also requires a strategic approach to lead generation and qualification to ensure success.

This chapter will guide you through the steps necessary to attract, qualify, and engage with potential clients effectively.

2.0

Generating & Qualifying Leads

Executive Summary

To generate leads and engage potential clients as an architect or interior designer, start by sparking curiosity and positioning yourself as a knowledgeable resource. Initiate conversations around shared interests, subtly steering them toward your expertise. When asked, "What do you do?" introduce your profession and unique services, highlighting the value you bring. Tailor your approach by researching clients' preferences, needs, and dislikes, crafting personalized proposals that demonstrate dedication and build trust. Show genuine interest in their vision, and explain how your designs can enhance their lives, transforming casual interest into qualified leads.

Create a sense of urgency by aligning their desires with broader needs and emphasizing the benefits of working with you. Treat every client with equal passion, regardless of project size, as each interaction provides valuable insights for future work. Actively listen to clients, incorporating their cues into tailored solutions that resonate deeply. This approach not only secures projects but also fosters word-of-mouth referrals and long-term relationships.

By focusing on adding value, demonstrating expertise, and maintaining a positive attitude, you can master the art of sales in interior design. Consistent practice sharpens your skills, encourages innovation, and ensures sustained success in attracting and retaining ideal clients.

2.1

Ways to Attract the Right Clients: Marketing, Referrals, and Networking

Attracting the **ideal client** is foundational to success in interior design. In India, where design preferences, budgets, and lifestyles vary widely, it's critical to define and target the **right segment** of the population that aligns with your expertise and style. For instance, a designer specializing in modern, minimalist designs would target different clients than one focusing on traditional, luxury interiors.

Marketing Strategies for Indian Interior Designers:

1. **Online Presence**: Having a strong digital presence is critical. As of 2023, India had over **692 million internet users**, with many potential clients turning to platforms like Instagram, Pinterest, and Houzz for design inspiration. **Social media marketing** is a powerful tool for designers to showcase their portfolios, build a brand, and attract clients. Sharing high-quality images of past projects, before-and-after transformations, and engaging with followers through polls and Q&A sessions helps to **build credibility** and attract attention.

2. **SEO and Website Optimization**: A professional website optimized for **search engines** is essential. Clients often search for "best interior designers in [city name]" on Google. Incorporating **local SEO strategies** can help attract clients in specific locations. Additionally, **blogging** about design trends, tips for homeowners, or case studies from your projects can improve visibility and establish authority in your niche.

3. **Referrals and Word-of-Mouth**: In India, the **word-of-mouth referral system** remains one of the most powerful forms of marketing, especially in the interior design field where personal recommendations carry significant weight. Encouraging satisfied clients to recommend your services to others and offering referral incentives (e.g., discounts on future services) can be highly effective.

4. **Networking with Industry Professionals**: Building relationships with real estate developers, architects, and furniture vendors can provide a steady source of leads. These professionals often need to recommend interior designers to their clients, making strategic partnerships critical.

5. **Showcasing at Local Exhibitions**: In cities like Mumbai, Delhi, and Bangalore, design exhibitions and home fairs are popular platforms where interior designers can showcase their work and directly interact with potential clients. Events such as **India Design ID** and **ACETECH** offer opportunities to network and generate leads.

Key Point: Combining **digital marketing** with **local networking** and **referrals** is essential for interior designers in India, where personal recommendations often hold more weight than advertisements. Having a digital presence is a must for any professional these days.

2.2

The Right Questions to Qualify Leads

Not all leads are equal, and one of the most important skills for a designer is to **qualify leads** early to ensure they are worth pursuing. This involves identifying whether a potential client aligns with your services, budget expectations, and project scope.

Key Questions to Ask During Initial Contact:

1. **What is the scope of your project?** – Understanding the size and complexity of the project is essential. Is it a single-room renovation, a new build, or a full home redesign?

2. **What is your budget?** – Discussing budget early on is critical. According to research, **approximately 42% of project failures are due to budget misalignment** . In the Indian market, where costs can vary drastically between cities and types of homes, having a clear idea of what the client can afford helps set realistic expectations.

3. **What is your timeline?** – Indian clients often expect rapid turnarounds due to festival seasons, wedding timelines, or moving into new homes during auspicious times. Understanding their timeline can help you gauge whether the project is feasible within their expectations.

4. **What is your design style or vision?** – Ask the client about their preferred design style, materials, and finishes. If your design philosophy doesn't align with theirs (e.g., if they want traditional design but you specialize in modern aesthetics), it's better to identify this early.

Key Point: Asking the right questions early saves time by filtering out clients who may not be a good fit, allowing you to focus on high-value opportunities.

2.3

High-Value Leads vs. Low-Priority Inquiries

Once you've gathered preliminary information from a potential client, the next step is to filter high-value leads from low-priority ones. High-value leads are those that fit your design expertise, budget range, and timeline. They are also more likely to align with your creative vision and have a genuine interest in a long-term partnership. Prioritizing these leads ensures you can focus your energy and resources on projects that maximize your impact and professional growth.

Criteria for High-Value Leads:

- **Alignment with Your Services**: Does the client's project fit within your areas of expertise? For example, if your specialty is designing contemporary homes but the client wants a traditional Indian aesthetic with heavy use of woodwork and intricate detailing, this might not be an ideal match.

- **Budget Fit**: Does the client have a budget that aligns with the quality of work you provide? In major cities like Mumbai and Delhi, interior design costs can range from **INR 1,500 to INR 3,000 per square foot**, depending on materials and labor costs . If the client's budget is far below this, you may need to adjust expectations or suggest alternative solutions.

- **Timeline Compatibility**: A high-value lead is also one that fits within your project timeline. If you're booked for months ahead and the client needs immediate work, it may be better to pass on the lead rather than risk client dissatisfaction.

- **Long-Term Potential**: High-value clients often represent opportunities for repeat business or referrals. **Property developers, for instance, may offer multiple projects** if the first collaboration is successful.

Key Point: Filtering your leads helps you avoid overcommitting and allows you to focus on projects where you can deliver the most value.`

2.4

Best Ways to Approach Leads: Phone Call, Emails, Social Media Messages

The **first contact** with a lead is crucial, as it sets the tone for the rest of the relationship. The initial approach should be **professional, clear, and engaging**.

- **Phone Call**: A phone conversation allows for a more personal touch. During the call, introduce yourself, explain your services, and ask about the project scope and budget. It's important to establish rapport and **listen carefully** to what the client needs.

- **Emails**: An introductory email should be professional and concise. Include a brief introduction to your services, examples of past projects (attach a **portfolio PDF** or include links), and ask for more details about their project. Be sure to include a **call-to-action** to schedule a consultation.

- **Social Media Messages**: Many clients may first contact you via social media platforms like Instagram or Facebook. Respond promptly and professionally, and move the conversation to phone or email for a more detailed discussion. Social media is a **good platform for initial engagement**, but follow-up should happen in a more formal setting.

Key Point: The first contact is your chance to **make a strong impression** and begin building trust with the client. Be professional, responsive, and inquisitive.

2.5

Scheduling the First Consultation: Creating an Engaging and Productive First Meeting

The **initial consultation** is a critical part of the sales process, as it allows you to meet the client in person (or virtually) and dive deeper into their needs, preferences, and project details.

Key Considerations for a Productive Consultation:

- **Preparation**: Before the consultation, review the information you've gathered from the client and prepare relevant materials, such as examples of past work, design inspirations, and potential solutions.

- **Structured Agenda**: Have a structured agenda to guide the conversation. This could include discussing the client's vision, budget, timeline, and any constraints.

- **Listening First**: This meeting should focus on **active listening**. Let the client speak about their goals, lifestyle, and expectations. Ask clarifying questions, and take detailed notes.

- **Preliminary Ideas**: Offer some preliminary design ideas, but avoid going too deep into the design at this stage. The goal is to **build rapport** and gather more information before providing a concrete proposal.

Key Point: The first meeting should focus on understanding the client's needs and laying the groundwork for a productive working relationship.

2.6

Identifying Red Flags in Leads

While every lead represents an opportunity, it's important to recognize potential **red flags** that could indicate a problematic client or project. Here are some common red flags:

- **Unrealistic Budget Expectations**: If a client insists on a luxurious design but has an unrealistically low budget, this is a sign of potential friction. It's essential to educate clients early on about what their budget can realistically achieve.

- **Ambiguous Project Scope**: If the client is vague about the project's scope or changes their requirements frequently, this could lead to issues later in the project.

- **Unreasonable Timelines**: Some clients may expect projects to be completed within impossibly short timeframes. If this is the case, it's important to **set realistic expectations** from the beginning.

- **Difficulty in Communication**: If a client is unresponsive or unclear in their communication during the lead generation phase, this could lead to bigger problems once the project begins.

Key Point: Identifying red flags early on helps avoid potential conflicts and ensures a smoother, more productive client-designer relationship.

Tool 2.7

Lead Capture Form for Initial Inquiries

The **Lead Capture Form** is used when potential clients reach out via your website, social media, or other channels. This form allows you to collect essential information upfront so that you can respond efficiently and schedule the next steps. During follow up call, they can use the Lead Qualification Checklist to ask targeted questions, assess the project's viability, and determine the fit with their design expertise.

Section	Client Input
Name	
Phone & Email	
Project Type	Full home design ☐ Room redesign ☐ Kitchen/bathroom renovation ☐ Other ☐
Location of the Project	City/Area:
Preferred Design Style	Modern ☐ Traditional ☐ Contemporary ☐ Minimalist ☐ Eclectic ☐ Other ☐
Approximate Budget for the Project	Below INR 5 lac ☐ INR 5 lac - 10 lac ☐ INR 10 lac - 20 lac ☐ INR 20 lac and above ☐
Desired Start and Completion Date	
Key Objectives/Challenges	What do you want to achieve with this project? (e.g., space optimization, complete transformation, minor updates)
Any Special Requirements	(e.g., eco-friendly materials, accessibility, etc.)
Have you worked with an interior designer before?	Yes ☐ No ☐ If yes, how was your experience?
Next Steps	
Would you be available for an initial consultation?	Yes ☐ No ☐
Additional Comments/Questions	

Table 2.1 : Lead Capturing Form

Tool 2.8

Lead Qualification Checklist

This checklist is a tool for designers to qualify leads effectively. It includes targeted questions to evaluate the project's scope, budget, and timeline. By addressing these areas, designers can gauge the viability of the opportunity. It also helps determine whether the project aligns with their design expertise.

Criteria	Question to Ask	Response	Qualify (Y/N)
Project Scope	What is the scope of the project? (e.g., full home redesign, one-room makeover, renovation, etc.)		
Design Style Preference	What is your preferred design style? (e.g., modern, traditional, eclectic, minimalistic)		
Budget	What is your approximate budget for the project? (Ask for a specific range)		
Timeline	When are you hoping to start and complete the project?		
Decision Makers	Who will be making the final decisions on this project?		
Experience with Designers	Have you worked with an interior designer before? If yes, what was the experience like?		
Special Requirements	Do you have any specific requirements or challenges that need to be addressed? (e.g., sustainable design, space optimization, family needs, etc.)		
Project Location	Where is the project located? (city, remote area)		
Availability for Meeting	Are you available for an initial consultation to discuss further?		

Table 2.2 : Lead Qualification Checklist

Conclusion

Generating and qualifying leads is a critical aspect of the sales process for interior designers. By using effective marketing strategies, asking the right questions early, and qualifying leads based on budget, scope, and expectations, designers can focus their efforts on high-value clients and deliver successful projects.

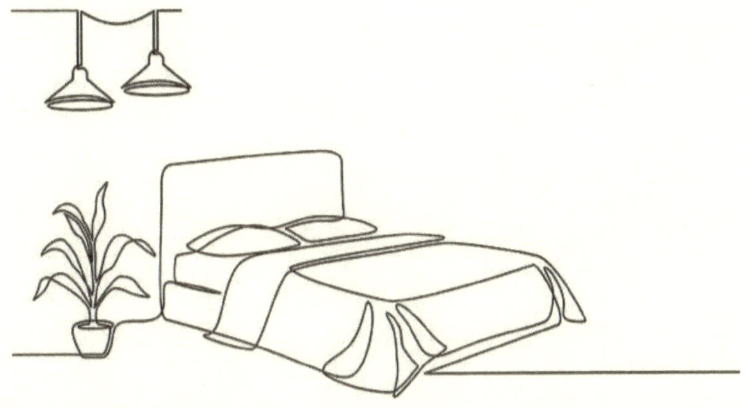

3.

The Art of Understanding Clients

3.1 Defining Client Persona

3.2 Types of Residential Interior Clients

3.3 Demographics, Lifestyle, and Design Needs

3.4 Identifying Client Motivation: The X-Factor

3.5 Building Client Persona Template

3.6 Read and Respond to Client Responses

Tools & Formats:

3.7 Sample of Client Persona

3.8 Sample Solution Post Persona Mapping

Scan here
for more
digital
content

3.0

The Art of Understanding Clients

Executive Summary

In residential interior design, the relationship between designer and client is paramount. Successful interior design is not just about aesthetics; it is about crafting a space that reflects the client's needs, lifestyle, and personality. To achieve this, interior designers must understand their clients deeply, and this is where the concept of "Client Persona Mapping" comes into play.

Mapping client personas allows designers to profile their clients based on various attributes, helping them tailor design solutions that align with client expectations and preferences. In India, where residential design is growing rapidly, understanding the diversity of client types, from first-time homeowners to luxury clients, is crucial.

3.1

Defining Client Persona: Why Does It Matter?

A **client persona** is a semi-fictional representation of a designer's ideal client, based on data about their demographics, behaviors, needs, and goals. While the concept of personas is widely used in marketing and product development, its application in interior design is relatively underexplored.

However, understanding client personas is equally important for interior designers, as it provides a structured way to anticipate client preferences, behaviors, and pain points.

Why It Matters:

- **Personalization**: With client personas, interior designers can create spaces that are more tailored to the individual, enhancing client satisfaction.

- **Efficiency**: By understanding client types, designers can streamline the decision-making process, presenting solutions that fit the client's needs from the outset.

- **Communication**: Personas help designers communicate more effectively, using language and design references that resonate with the client.

Internationally, renowned designers like **Kelly Hoppen** have emphasized the importance of understanding the client's "inner vision" to deliver successful designs. Hoppen's emphasis on "tailored luxury" and functional aesthetics stems from a deep understanding of her client's aspirations and lifestyle, a practice that can be structured through persona mapping.

3.2

Types of Residential Interior Clients

Indian residential clients vary widely in terms of their motivations, design preferences, and budget capacities. Understanding these distinct client types can significantly influence how a designer approaches a project. Below are four key client personas relevant to the Indian market:

3.2.1

First-time Homeowners

First-time homeowners in India typically seek **affordable and functional** designs. These clients are often young professionals or newlyweds, working within a limited budget but eager to make their space aesthetically pleasing. They may be influenced by popular trends on social media platforms such as Instagram and Pinterest. Their focus is usually on practicality, space optimization, and adding personal touches within a **mid-range budget**.

- **Key Needs**: Cost-effective design, storage solutions, space optimization, easy-to-maintain materials, multi-functional furniture

- **Design Preference**: Minimalistic, contemporary, or Scandinavian styles, Neutral or soft color palettes (Tier-1 cities)

- **Challenges**: Budget constraints, lack of experience with design processes, limited understanding of material durability

3.2.2

Luxury Clients

At the opposite end of the spectrum, **luxury clients** expect high-end, bespoke designs that reflect their status. These clients often have experience working with designers and value the exclusivity of custom pieces, premium materials, and high-end craftsmanship. Internationally, luxury clients look for iconic names in interior design, such as **Peter Marino**, whose work with brands like Chanel reflects a deep understanding of luxury design. In India, the luxury market is expanding, especially in metropolitan areas like Mumbai and Delhi. These clients often prefer designs that incorporate **luxurious materials** such as marble, exotic woods, and designer furniture, often combining global influences with local aesthetics.

- **Key Needs**: Exclusivity, bespoke design, luxurious materials

- **Design Preference**: Modern luxury, eclectic, fusion of traditional and contemporary elements

- **Challenges**: High expectations, coordination with international suppliers, time-intensive project

3.2.3

Renovators and Upgraders

This group consists of clients who are either renovating their existing homes or upgrading specific spaces, such as kitchens or bathrooms. These clients often have a **clear vision** based on past experiences but may seek guidance in modernizing their home or adding value to their property. They are typically mid to high-budget clients who prioritize quality and long-term solutions. Many are looking for designs that balance functionality with a refreshed aesthetic, reflecting current trends.

- **Key Needs**: Incorporating modern elements while retaining the home's original character

- **Design Preference**: Transitional design, mix of traditional and contemporary styles

- **Challenges**: Balancing new design with existing architecture, managing partial renovations

3.2.4

Investors and Property Developers

Real estate investors and developers often engage interior designers for **property staging** or designing show flats to attract buyers. These clients are primarily driven by **return on investment (ROI)** and seek designs that can increase property value. Unlike other clients, they tend to be less emotionally attached to the project and are more focused on market trends and buyer appeal.

They usually prefer cost-effective yet visually impactful solutions that appeal to a broad audience. Timely delivery is critical, as delays can directly impact their project timelines and profitability.

- **Key Needs**: Marketable designs that appeal to potential buyers, quick project turnaround

- **Design Preference**: Neutral, market-appealing styles that are on-trend but not too niche

- **Challenges**: Tight deadlines, working within budget constraints to maximize ROI

3.3

Demographics, Lifestyle, and Design Needs

When building client personas, it is essential to delve into both **demographic** and **psychographic** information. Demographic data includes attributes like age, income, and family structure, while psychographics involve more nuanced aspects like personality, values, and lifestyle preferences. In India, where cultural diversity and regional influences shape lifestyles, these factors become especially significant.

- **Demographic Insights**: For example, clients in their 30s in urban centers like Mumbai may prefer modern, minimalist designs with smart home features, whereas clients in their 50s from tier-2 cities may opt for more traditional aesthetics, emphasizing comfort and family-oriented spaces.

- **Psychographic Insights**: Understanding a client's values and lifestyle choices can help in defining the design approach. For instance, eco-conscious clients may prioritize **sustainable materials**, while technology enthusiasts may want **smart home integration**.

An academic reference to psychographic data in design is the concept of **Maslow's Hierarchy of Needs**, where the design of a space can cater to various psychological and emotional needs of clients, such as safety, belonging, and self-expression.

3.4

Identifying Client Motivation: The X-Factor !

Functionality, Aesthetics, or Value-Driven?

Clients approach interior design with various **motivations**, and understanding these can greatly influence the success of a project. Typically, clients fall into one of three categories:

- **Functionality-Driven Clients**: These clients prioritize the usability and efficiency of their spaces. For instance, first-time homeowners often focus on practical aspects like storage solutions and space management. Understanding their motivation allows designers to emphasize **space-saving techniques** and **multi-functional furniture**.

- **Aesthetics-Driven Clients**: These clients value the **visual appeal** of their spaces and often have specific design preferences. Luxury clients, for example, may be driven by the desire for uniqueness and exclusivity, which means emphasizing high-end finishes and custom-made furniture in your design pitch.

- **Value-Driven Clients**: Investors or renovators are more focused on the **return on investment** or increasing property value. The design approach for these clients should highlight how certain design choices, such as upgraded kitchens or bathrooms, can enhance resale value.

- **Sustainability-Conscious Clients:** These clients prioritize eco-friendly materials, energy-efficient solutions, and sustainable design practices. They appreciate features like recycled materials, solar panels, and low-VOC paints, making it essential to present green alternatives in your proposal.

- **Experience-Seeking Clients:** Some clients are motivated by a desire to create a specific mood or experience in their space, such as a spa-like bathroom, a high-tech entertainment lounge, or a cozy, hygge-inspired home. Understanding their lifestyle and emotional goals allows for a more tailored design approach.

Identifying Client Motivations:

- Ask targeted questions: "What challenges are you currently facing with your space?" "Are there specific areas where functionality is more important to you, such as storage or workflow?" "What would make your day-to-day life easier in this space?"

- Observe their lifestyle and decision-making process to understand whether they prioritize practicality, aesthetics, or cost-effectiveness.

- Analyze their engagement with design elements—do they focus on mood boards and material samples (aesthetic-driven) or ask about durability and practicality (functionality-driven)?

- Assess their past design experiences, if any, to gauge what worked or didn't in previous projects.

Key Point: Aligning design solutions with the client's core motivations or in other words X-Factors ensures greater client satisfaction and a smoother design process

3.5

Building a Client Persona Template

A **client persona template** is a structured framework that allows designers to collect and organize information about their clients systematically. Below is a simplified version of a client persona template for interior designers:

Section	Details
Client Name/Type	Example: "First-time Homeowner" or "Luxury Client"
Age Group	Example: 25-35, 40-50
Income Range	Example: INR 10,00,000 - 20,00,000 per annum
Location	Example: Mumbai (Urban), Bangalore (Suburban)
Family Structure	Example: Married couple with two children
Occupation	Example: IT Professional, Doctor, Entrepreneur
Lifestyle Preferences	Example: Busy professionals seeking low-maintenance, space-efficient design
Key Motivations	Example: Functionality, cost-effective design, child-friendly environment
Style Preferences	Example: Modern, Minimalist, Contemporary
Budget Expectations	Example: INR 8,00,000 - 12,00,000
Safety Measures	Example: home need to be equipped with alarm
Desired Timeline	Example: Project start in Apr, complete by Sep
Decision Makers	Example: Husband and wife making decisions together
Design Challenges	Example: Small space, requires clever storage solutions
Additional Notes	Example: Clients are tech-savvy and interested in smart home features

Table 3.1 : Client Persona Template

3.6.

Read and Respond to Client Responses:

1. **Project Type and Scope**: If a client requests a full home design, they expect a cohesive theme throughout the house. On the other hand, a room redesign narrows the focus to a single space. Designers should adapt their planning and allocate resources accordingly. Smaller projects allow for more detail in individual spaces, while larger projects require broader conceptualization.

2. **Location and Space**: Urban clients often face space constraints, especially in cities like Mumbai or Delhi. In response, designers should prioritize **space optimization methods** like foldable furniture or hidden storage. Suburban homes typically have more space, which allows for **larger, statement furniture** and more open layouts.

3. **Lifestyle and Family Structure**: For families with children, focus on safety, durability, and practicality. This includes using **stain-resistant materials** and avoiding sharp edges. If the household includes elderly members, consider accessibility features such as **non-slip flooring** and ergonomic designs.

4. **Budget Management**: A mid-range budget requires careful material selection, where cost-effective solutions are used in less visible areas, and high-quality materials are reserved for statement pieces. If the budget increases, **premium materials** and custom furniture can be added to enhance luxury. If the budget decreases, **focus on value-engineering** to maintain style without sacrificing quality.

5. **Timeline**: Timelines significantly impact the scope of the project. If the client's timeline is tight, the designer may need to use **off-the-shelf products** instead of custom-made options or consider **phasing the project** to deliver parts of it earlier.

6. **Design Style**: A modern, minimalist style focuses on functionality, clean lines, and minimal clutter. If the client's style shifts to **traditional or eclectic**, the designer can introduce **rich textures, warmer colors**, and **decorative elements** like moldings and detailed craftsmanship.

7. **Special Requirements and Preferences**: Client preferences, such as a desire for **custom furniture** or **smart home integration**, require collab with specialists (local artisans or tech integrators).

3.7.

Sample Client Persona : A Couple Looking for Smart Kitchen

Introduction : Rahul & Ratna	Brief with End Goals	
Address : 506, Sky Marina Sukhadia Circle, Bangalore Ph: 997160XXXX Email : rrs@XXXX.com	Kitchen Purpose	: Personal Use
	Kitchen Scope	: New Modular
	Kitchen Size	: 8' x 10'
Scenario A couple deeply engrossed in their work-life, Ratna and Rahul are all geared up for their new home. They want a modern so that they can enjoy stirring some comfort food in whatever time they can spare from work. **A smart kitchen with kids safety is the term excite them to have one."**	Kitchen Shape	: L Shape
	Primary User	: Owner
	Secondary User	: Owner
	Uses Weekdays	: Regular
	Uses Weekend	: Moderate
	Consumable Load	: Moderate
Demographic Profile:	Non Consumable	: Moderate
Personal : Rahul is born and brought up in Bengaluru, married to Ratna from Pune. Kids Hanna & Ananya 6 & 5 Years age. Recently bought a 2 BHK flat with help of joint loan. After 7-8 year of rented home life, now both need a real smart kitchen suit to their personality and lifestyle. Ranta likes to cook hence she prefer no domestic help in kitchen for cooking but yes for cleaning.	Accessibility	: Default
	Convenient	: Default
	Automation	**: Heavy**
	Multi Utility	: Yes
	Maintenance	: Moderate
	Cultural Impact	: Moderate
Profession : Rahul is a IT professional at senior level and Ratna works for Insurance company as executive. Both has 5 days on the go working life and combined package is approx 45 to 50 lac ctc per annum.	**Kids Safety**	**: Yes**
	Design Style	: Modern
	Color Palate	: Netural
	Handle Preference	: Handleless
	Color Preference	: Pure White
Social : 2-3 times in month family eats out and similarly 2-3 time invite friends or family at home. 10-12 people's is the max gathering including kids.	Finish Preference	: Matt + Gloss
	Budget	: 5-6 Lac
	Timeline	: 45 Days

Tool 3.8

Sample Solution Post Persona Mapping

Smart Kitchen for Young Professionals in Bangalore

Client Context: Rahul and Ratna, a career-driven couple in their mid-30s, recently purchased a 2BHK apartment in Bangalore after spending 7-8 years in rented homes. With demanding five-day work schedules, Rahul, a Senior IT Professional, and Ratna, an Insurance Executive, sought a modern, smart, and highly functional kitchen that aligned with their fast-paced lifestyle. While Ratna enjoys cooking and prefers not to have domestic help for meal preparation, she values a well-organized, low-maintenance kitchen that simplifies daily tasks.

With two young children, Hanna (6) and Ananya (5), the couple prioritized child safety, smart automation, and efficient storage solutions. Their home frequently hosts family and friends (10-12 guests), making a seamless, clutter-free, and multi-functional kitchen essential for both daily cooking and occasional entertaining.

Client Priorities:

- **Smart & Efficient Kitchen:** A tech-integrated space with smart lighting, voice-controlled appliances, and touch-free faucets to enhance convenience and efficiency.

- **Low Maintenance:** Easy-to-clean surfaces, durable materials, and an organized layout to reduce daily upkeep, accommodating their busy work schedules.

- **Child Safety:** A kitchen designed with soft-close cabinets, rounded edges, child-lock appliances, and safe cooking zones for their young children, Hanna (6) and Ananya (5).

- **Optimized Storage & Accessibility:** Pull-out pantry units, concealed storage, and modular cabinets to keep essentials within easy reach while maintaining a clutter-free aesthetic.

- **Multi-Functional Space:** A foldable breakfast counter for quick meals, a dining area that doubles as a workspace, and efficient zoning for meal prep and entertaining.

- **Seamless Aesthetic:** A modern, handleless kitchen with a neutral color palette (pure white, matte + gloss finish) that reflects sophistication and simplicity.

- **Budget & Timeline Compliance:** Execution within ₹5-6 lakh and completion within 45 days, ensuring a smooth transition into their new home.

Design Solution (Post Persona Mapping):

The designer utilized **persona mapping** to gain deeper insights into the couple's lifestyle, identifying the following needs:

- **Smart Kitchen Integration:** The kitchen was designed with sensor-based lighting, touch-free faucets, and voice-controlled appliances to make cooking seamless. An automated chimney and built-in exhaust were added for improved ventilation.

- **Space Optimization & Storage:** Since Ratna prefers an organized, clutter-free space, the kitchen included modular pull-out storage, concealed cabinets, and vertical organizers to maximize efficiency.

- **Multi-Functional Features:** A foldable breakfast counter was incorporated for quick meals and casual dining. The tall unit storage ensured bulk groceries could be stored with ease.

- **Child-Safe Features:** To ensure kids' safety, soft-close cabinets, rounded edges, and induction cooking with child-lock features were installed.

- **Aesthetic & Practical Balance:** The handleless design, a neutral white color scheme, and a mix of matte and gloss finishes created a sleek yet easy-to-maintain kitchen.

- **Timely Handover:** With a limited timeline, efficient project management ensures on-time delivery while keeping the budget under control.

Outcome:

The kitchen was completed within 45 days, staying within the ₹5-6 lakh budget. The smart automation significantly improved their daily routine, allowing hands-free cooking, easy maintenance, and remote-controlled appliances. The seamless, clutter-free design made the space efficient yet inviting.

Delighted with the transformation, Rahul and Ratna referred the designer to their colleagues, leading to multiple new projects and reinforcing the success of persona-driven kitchen design.

Conclusion:

This chapter has provided an in-depth look at how client personas can be developed and used effectively, drawing from both international design practices and the unique attributes of the Indian residential design market. By understanding a client's lifestyle, priorities, and functional needs, designers can create spaces that are not only aesthetically pleasing but also practical and personalized. A well-defined persona helps in making informed design decisions, ensuring that every element—from material selection to smart technology integration—is aligned with the client's expectations. Furthermore, persona-driven design enhances client satisfaction, leading to positive referrals and long-term business growth. As the interior design industry evolves, mastering this approach will empower designers to offer tailored solutions, making their work more impactful and successful.

4.

Building Rapport and Trust

4.1 Setting the Right Tone in Meetings

4.2 The Role of Active Listening in Client Conversations

4.3 Showing Empathy to Understand Client Stress

4.4 Positioning Yourself as a Consultant

4.5 Establishing Confidence in Your Expertise

4.6 Building Long-Term Trust with Honesty

Tools & Formats:

4.7 First Meeting Agenda Template

4.8 Follow-up Email Template

Scan here
for more
digital
content

4.0

Building Rapport and Trust

Executive Summary

Building a strong rapport with clients is essential for interior designers, especially when working on residential projects where clients are often emotionally invested in the outcome. Trust is the cornerstone of any client-designer relationship, and establishing it early is crucial to the project's success.

Clients need to feel that their designer not only understands their vision but can also guide them through the design process with expertise and empathy. This chapter explores how interior designers can build trust by positioning themselves as consultants and establishing meaningful relationships based on transparency, active listening, and credibility.

4.1

Setting the Right Tone in Meetings

The first client meeting is critical in establishing the tone, trust and direction of the entire project. Research shows that first impressions are often formed within the first seven seconds of greeting, meeting and interaction, emphasizing the importance of professionalism and preparation from the outset .

This initial meeting is not only about exchanging information but also about building trust and ensuring that both the client and designer are on the same page regarding requirements, expectations, vision, timeline and workflow.

Key Actions to Set the Right Tone:

- **Preparation**: Before the first meeting, familiarize yourself with the client's preferences (from the lead qualification and discovery forms), review their project requirements, and bring a curated selection of past work that aligns with their vision. This level of preparation shows professionalism and attention to detail.

- **Warm Welcome**: Begin the meeting with a friendly, professional greeting, creating a comfortable and open atmosphere. Designers like **Kelly Wearstler** emphasize that every client interaction should start by making clients feel valued and respected, setting the stage for productive collaboration.

- **Clear Agenda**: Having a **first meeting agenda** (discussed in Tools & Formats section in detail) will provide structure to the meeting, ensuring that all relevant points are discussed and the client feels that their time is respected. The agenda should include an introduction, an overview of the client's needs, a discussion of the design process, budget, and next steps.

Key Point: The first meeting is your opportunity to build trust, a factor that is critical in the **client-designer relationship**. A survey by the **American Society of Interior Designers (ASID)** revealed that clients who felt respected and valued in their initial meeting were 30% more likely to recommend the designer to others . This underscores the importance of getting the first meeting right—not just to win the current project but also to build a network of future clients.

4.2

The Role of Active Listening in Client Conversations

One of the most critical skills for an interior designer is **active listening**. While designers are often focused on bringing their creative vision to life, the first priority should always be to **understand the client's needs and desires**. Active listening involves not just carefully hearing the words and requirements but understanding the meaning behind them, allowing the designer to grasp unspoken concerns, preferences, or hesitations.

How to Practice Active Listening:

- **Focus**: Give the client your full attention by maintaining eye contact, nodding, and responding to cues. Avoid distractions, such as checking your phone or interrupting the client mid-sentence.

- **Paraphrase and Clarify**: After the client expresses their thoughts, paraphrase their main points to ensure you've understood them correctly.

  Example: "It sounds like you're looking for a design that feels modern but still has some cozy, traditional elements. Is that right?"

- **Non-Verbal Cues**: Pay attention to the client's body language and tone of voice. Clients might not always articulate their concerns directly, but through observation, you can pick up on hesitation or enthusiasm about specific ideas.

  Example: A client may verbally agree to a color scheme but seem hesitant or uncomfortable in their body language (e.g., crossed arms or averted eye contact). The designer can ask, "I noticed you're not too excited about the color palette. We can relook the schement. Are there other options you'd like to explore?" This not only reassures the client but also opens up a deeper conversation about their preferences.

Internationally recognized designers, such as **Nate Berkus**, have emphasized that the best projects result from deep collaboration, which can only happen when the designer fully understands the client's vision.

Key Point: Active listening builds trust by showing that you value the client's input and are committed to designing a space that reflects their true needs and preferences.

4.3

Showing Empathy to Understand Client Stress

Residential interior design projects often involve high levels of client stress due to personal, financial, and emotional investments in the project. Designers must show empathy by acknowledging these pressures and demonstrating that they are there to support and guide clients through the process.

Ways to Show Empathy:

- **Acknowledge the Client's Concerns**: Whether it's budget, timelines, or design outcomes, it's essential to recognize the sources of stress for your client. This builds a sense of partnership.

- **Be Patient**: Clients may change their minds, express frustration, or feel overwhelmed by choices. Demonstrating patience shows that you are committed to the long-term success of the project.

- **Offer Reassurance**: Empathy also involves providing reassurance that any issues can be worked through. For instance, if the client is worried about costs, quality, timeline, reassure them by offering alternative options that maintain the design's integrity while staying within budget.

Example: If the client is worried about exceeding their budget, the designer could reassure them by saying, "There are plenty of ways to achieve a similar look without increasing costs. I'll show you some materials and finishes that are more budget-friendly but still high quality." This allows the client to feel supported while still maintaining the integrity of the design.

In India, where emotional investments in homes interiors discussions are often high due to cultural significance, clients may be particularly sensitive to design decisions. Designer **Gauri Khan** has emphasized the importance of building relationships based on trust and understanding emotions, which ultimately leads to more meaningful and satisfying design solutions. *(Source: Interview with Gauri Khan, Architectural Digest India, 2019).*

Key Point: Showing empathy not only strengthens the client-designer bond but also fosters a sense of security, helping clients feel confident in their choices and in your ability to manage their concerns.

4.4

Positioning Yourself as a Consultant

Interior designers are not simply selling services; they are offering **expert consultation** that adds value to the client's home and lifestyle. This shift from "salesperson" to "consultant" is essential in building long-term trust with clients.

Ways to Position Yourself as a Consultant:

- **Solution-Oriented Conversations**: Instead of pushing specific design ideas or products, focus on solving the client's problems. Ask questions that identify challenges, such as "What part of your current space doesn't work for you?" and then offer thoughtful solutions.

- **Educational Approach**: Clients often don't understand the intricacies of design, such as material choices, layouts, or costs. A consultant explains these aspects, guiding the client through decisions. For example, if a client is debating between two flooring options, explain the pros and cons of each in terms of durability, maintenance, and cost.

  Example: If a client is debating between **hardwood** and **vinyl plank flooring**, the designer might explain, "Hardwood gives a classic, high-end look but requires more maintenance, while vinyl offers similar aesthetics with better water resistance and easier upkeep, especially in high-traffic areas." This educative approach empowers the client to make a choice that best fits their lifestyle.

- **Client-Centered Solutions**: A consultant listens to the client's vision and works with them to shape it, rather than imposing their own preferences. As **Joanna Gaines** famously said, "It's your house; it should look like you," emphasizing the importance of tailoring designs to the client rather than imposing the designer's own aesthetic.

- **Value-Driven Recommendations:** Instead of simply suggesting premium materials or costly upgrades, focus on value-based recommendations that align with the client's priorities.

Key Point: Positioning yourself as a consultant helps you build trust and authority. Clients see that you are invested in their goals, equipped with the experience to address diverse needs and solutions, and not just focused on your own vision or revenue.

4.4.1

Steps to implement the Consultative Approach

The consultative approach does not focus on short-term sales win, fulfilling requests that bring temporary happiness like discount or offer or relying on our clients to drive strategy; it needs to take a more structured approach. The recommendation to implement this approach are:

- **Ask Questions:** Asking plenty of open-ended questions with very nice tone to influence the client to volunteer critical information about their needs.
- **Get Response:** Active listening: restating and paraphrasing what clients tell in their own words to confirm understanding of what they're sharing about their needs.
- **Educate Impact:** Consistently educate the client through the sharing of key insights and takeaways. Explain the 'what and why' behind the suggested product or solution.
- **Derive Solution:** Focusing on deriving the overall solution with **"the big picture"**, which actually takes the customer's needs from current state to the desired state.

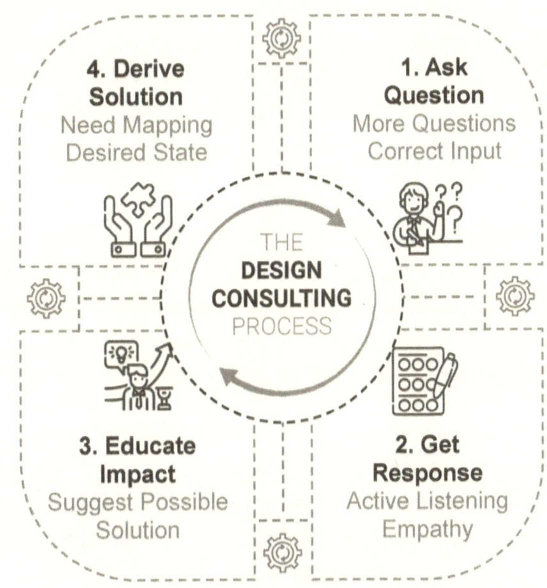

Illustration 4.1 : Steps to implement the Consultative Approach

Conclusion: The consultative approach is designed to put you in a position of being a trusted advisor to clients vs. merely being a salesperson or vendor. The deeper someone understands the client's need to solve their fundamental problems, the more valuable the whole consultation will be.

4.5

Establishing Confidence in Your Expertise

Clients need to feel confident that they are working with a professional who can deliver their vision while managing the complexities of a project. Creating confidence in your expertise requires a balance of **communication**, **credibility**, and **evidence of past success**.

Steps to Build Confidence in Your Expertise:

- **Share Past Successes**: During initial meetings, reference previous projects that align with the client's vision. Bring photos, testimonials, or case studies to demonstrate your ability to meet deadlines, manage budgets, and deliver high-quality designs.

- **Professional Certifications**: Highlight any relevant qualifications or certifications. In India, the **Institute of Indian Interior Designers (IIID)** is a well-recognized professional body. Mentioning membership, webinar attended or certifications from such institutions can enhance credibility.

- **Provide Clear Recommendations**: Confidence is built when clients trust that their designer knows what's best. After understanding their needs, offer firm recommendations and explain your reasoning. For instance, if they are unsure about a layout and placements, present a few options and explain why one is superior in terms of space efficiency or flow.

- **Collaborative Experience:** Showcasing your ability to collaborate with other professionals, such as architects, contractors, or suppliers, is essential. Clients want to know that you can handle the complexities of a project, which often involves coordinating with various stakeholders.

- **Demonstrating Thought Leadership:** Positioning yourself as a thought leader in the industry further solidifies your credibility. Whether it's publishing articles on design trends, speaking at industry conferences, or having a strong presence on platforms like **Houzz** or **Instagram**, showcasing your expertise publicly demonstrates that you are respected in the field.

Key Point: Clients will trust your recommendations when you back them up with clear reasoning, past experience, and demonstrated expertise.

4.6

Building Long-Term Trust with Honesty:

How to Build Long-Term Trust?

Transparency is one of the most important factors in establishing **long-term trust**. Clients need to know they can rely on you to be honest about costs, timelines, potential challenges, and the overall feasibility of their vision.

Principles of Transparency:

- **Be Honest About Budget**: Clients often have lofty aspirations that don't align with their budgets. Being honest about what is achievable within their financial constraints, while offering cost-effective alternatives, is essential. For example, explain the difference between premium and mid-range materials and how each affects the overall design and cost.

- **Discuss Potential Delays or Issues**: Don't shy away from addressing potential setbacks, whether related to supply chain delays, labor availability, short of delayed delivery or material sourcing. Clients will appreciate your honesty if issues arise, rather than feeling blindsided later.

  Example: *"The custom sofa you selected is perfect for your space, but there may be a 2-week delay in delivery due to the supplier's backlog. We can either wait for it, or I can suggest an alternative that is similar and available sooner. I'll keep you updated as soon as I hear more."*

- **Open Communication**: Keep clients informed every step of the way. Providing regular progress updates ensures clients never feel out of the loop and increases their confidence in your management of the project.

Designers like **Patricia Urquiola** emphasize the importance of open client communication, particularly in maintaining transparency about material sourcing and project timelines, which are often subject to delays or budget adjustments.

Key Point: Transparency eliminates potential misunderstandings, ensuring that clients trust you not only with the design but with their time and money.

Tool 4.7

First Meeting Agenda Template

The agenda template for the first client meeting is a key tool in ensuring a structured and productive conversation. It helps outline the main topics to be discussed, ensuring all essential areas are covered while respecting the client's time. By providing a clear framework, the agenda fosters transparency, builds trust, and aligns expectations between the designer and the client. Having this outline ensures both parties are on the same page, setting the stage for a successful partnership moving forward. Below is the template to capture agenda.

Agenda Item	Description
Welcome & Introduction	Introduce yourself and your team, and share an overview of your design philosophy and approach.
Project Overview	Invite the client to articulate their vision, objectives, and any challenges they anticipate, ensuring a clear understanding of their needs.
Design Process Overview	Provide a detailed explanation of your design process, including key phases, timelines, and milestones for the project.
Budget & Timeline Discussion	Discuss the client's budget, desired timeline, and any constraints to ensure alignment on expectations and feasibility.
Potential Challenges & Risk Factors	Address any potential challenges or risks in the project, such as site limitations, vendor availability, or unforeseen delays.
Communication	Establish communication protocols (e.g., frequency of updates, preferred methods of contact) to ensure smooth collaboration throughout the project.
Next Steps	Summarize the meeting, outline immediate next steps, and set expectations for follow-up actions, including additional information or meetings.

Table 4.1 : First Meeting Agenda Template

Tool 4.8

Follow-Up Email Template (Post-First Meeting)

A follow-up email after the first meeting is crucial for maintaining a professional connection, reinforcing key points discussed, and ensuring clarity around the next steps. It also provides an opportunity to show your attentiveness and commitment to the project.

Sending this email helps build trust and ensures both you and the client are aligned on expectations moving forward.

Following is the sample of email.

Subject: Great to Meet You! Next Steps for Your [Project Name]

Dear [Client Name],

It was a pleasure meeting with you today to discuss your vision for [brief description of the project]. I'm excited about the potential of working together and bringing your ideas to life.

Here's a quick recap of our discussion:

Project Scope: [Summarize key project elements]

Budget: [Client's budget expectations]

Timeline: [Agreed timeline or further discussion required]

Next Steps: [Mention any additional information needed from the client or a follow-up meeting]

I look forward to your thoughts and am happy to answer any questions or concerns you may have.

Thank you again for your time, and I look forward to continuing our conversation.

Best regards,
[Your Name]

Conclusion:

Building trust and rapport is a multi-faceted process that goes beyond merely selling design services. It involves active listening, empathy, transparency, and expert consultation. By positioning themselves as trusted consultants rather than salespeople, interior designers can foster stronger, longer-lasting client relationships that not only lead to successful projects but also to repeat business and referrals.

5.

Understanding Client Needs

5.1 Why Client Need Discovery is Crucial?

5.2 Conducting an In-Depth Client Needs Assessment

5.3 Functional Needs vs. Aesthetic Preferences

5.4 Understanding Financial and Budget Constraints

5.5 Balancing Emotional and Practical Needs in Design

5.6 Translating Client Desires into Concrete Design Concepts

Tools & Formats:

5.7 Client Needs Assessment Worksheet

5.8 Wish List vs. Must-Haves Worksheet

Scan here for more digital content

5.0

Understanding Client Needs

Executive Summary

Building upon the rapport established with the client, the next crucial step in the design process is conducting an in-depth client need analysis. This stage is vital for ensuring that the designer fully understands both the functional and emotional requirements of the project. It is not just about identifying surface-level preferences, but uncovering the deeper motivations and limitations that will guide the project. In India's growing interior design market, where the industry is expected to reach a valuation of INR 35,000 crore by 2025, effective need analysis is more critical than ever for delivering tailored, satisfying design solutions that meet clients' unique needs.

This chapter will explore the tools and techniques necessary for conducting a thorough client needs assessment, focusing on open-ended questioning, balancing aesthetic desires with functional needs, and ensuring the client's budget and practical limitations are respected throughout the process.

5.1

Why Client Need Discovery is Crucial?

Need discovery is the foundation of successful interior design. It goes beyond the initial discussions and is integral to creating a design that resonates with the client's lifestyle, values, and long-term expectations.

Without a proper understanding of the client's true needs, the designer runs the risk of creating a space that is visually appealing but functionally inadequate.

Why It Matters?

- **Personalization**: As designer **Nate Berkus** famously said, *"Your home should tell the story of who you are, and be a collection of what you love."* The need discovery process helps designers uncover what makes each client unique, allowing them to create spaces that are truly reflective of the client's personality.

- **Avoiding Misalignment**: Many projects fail not because of poor design, but due to a disconnect between what the client needs and what the designer delivers. In India, where clients often have specific cultural or practical requirements (such as **Vastu Shastra** compliance or multi-generational living spaces), understanding these needs is crucial for project success.

- **Client Satisfaction**: Studies suggest that **70% of project satisfaction** is based on how well the designer understood and met the client's needs, according to research by **DesignIntelligence**. Thus, effective need discovery can lead to higher client satisfaction and long-term client relationships.

5.2

Conducting an In-Depth Client Needs Assessment

The client needs assessment is a structured process that involves gathering detailed information about the client's vision, preferences, and constraints. It is an opportunity for the designer to dig deeper into the client's mindset and uncover both spoken and unspoken desires. By asking open-ended questions or by probing deeper to understand unspoken desires can be way to do such assessment successfully.

5.2.1

Asking Open-Ended Questions

Open-ended questions are designed to encourage the client to elaborate on their thoughts, rather than giving simple "yes" or "no" answers. This helps the designer gain a deeper understanding of the client's lifestyle, aspirations, and pain points.

Examples of Open-Ended Questions:

- **"How do you envision using this space on a daily basis?"**

  - This helps the designer understand functional needs and how the space will be utilized.

- **"What feeling do you want your home to evoke when you walk in?"**

  - This taps into the client's emotional desires, such as comfort, luxury, or warmth.

- **"What aspects of your current space don't work for you?"**

  - This question allows the client to express frustrations and problems with their existing layout, helping the designer avoid those mistakes in the new design.

5.2.2 How to Probe Deeper to Understand Unspoken Desires

Clients often have **latent needs** or desires they may not initially express. To uncover these, designers must employ probing techniques, asking follow-up questions that reveal deeper preferences.

Techniques for Probing Deeper:

- **Clarification**: If a client says they want a "modern" space, ask them to describe what "modern" means to them. The client may actually be referring to a minimalist, industrial, or mid-century modern aesthetic.

- **Challenge Assumptions**: If a client says, "I need more storage," probe further by asking, "What kind of items do you need to store, and where do you usually struggle with storage in your home?" This might reveal specific functional needs, like dedicated spaces for children's toys or work-from-home equipment.

- **Hypotheticals**: Pose hypothetical situations to the client to gauge their preferences.

For example, "If you had an unlimited budget, how would you transform this room?" This question can uncover hidden desires, even if they need to be scaled back for budgetary reasons.

5.3

Functional Needs vs. Aesthetic Preferences

A successful design must balance the **functional requirements** of the space with the **aesthetic preferences** of the client. Functionality refers to how the space works in terms of usability, while aesthetics relate to the visual and emotional appeal of the design.

Identifying Functional Needs:

- **Daily Use**: Spaces like kitchens and bathrooms often have strict functional requirements. For example, in many Indian homes, kitchens need to accommodate both traditional and modern cooking practices, which may involve large appliances and specific storage needs for spices and grains.

- **Space Planning**: In urban Indian areas like Mumbai or metro cities where space is limited or very costly, functional needs include **clever storage solutions**, multi-purpose furniture, and efficient layouts that maximize usability.

Identifying Aesthetic Preferences:

- **Style**: Clients may have specific stylistic preferences—modern, traditional, or eclectic. The designer should ensure that the chosen style reflects the client's personality and cultural background.

- **Cultural Influences**: In India, aesthetic preferences are often shaped by cultural practices. For example, **Vastu-compliant designs** are common requests in Indian homes, influencing everything from furniture placement to color schemes.

Balancing Function and Aesthetics:

According to **Elle Decor**, the most successful interiors are those where **functionality and aesthetics coexist harmoniously**.

For example, an aesthetically pleasing living room with impractical seating arrangements or insufficient lighting will not serve the client's needs, no matter how beautiful it looks.

5.4

Understanding Financial and Budget Constraints

Every design project comes with financial constraints, and it is crucial for the designer to manage the client's expectations within their budget. Understanding the budget early on helps prevent miscommunication, ensures the project remains feasible, and reduces the chances of cost overruns. Additionally, offering cost-effective alternatives can help maintain design integrity without exceeding financial limits.

Steps to Address Budget Constraints:

- **Define Budget Early**: Begin the discussion with a realistic understanding of what the client can spend. In Indian cities, the cost of a complete home interior can range from **INR 5 lakh to INR 20 lakh**, depending on the materials used and the scope of the project.

- **Offer Options**: Provide clients with a range of options—**budget-friendly**, **mid-range**, and **luxury solutions**. This allows them to make informed decisions about where they want to invest and where they are comfortable saving.

- **Be Transparent**: Share cost breakdowns for each element (furniture, finishes, labor) to help clients understand where their money is going. This transparency builds trust and keeps the project on track financially.

Key Point: Managing the client's budget with clarity and offering cost-effective alternatives ensures that the project stays within financial boundaries while still meeting design goals.

5.5

Balancing Emotional and Practical Needs in Design Solutions

Interior design is as much about emotion as it is about practicality. Clients seek spaces that evoke feelings of comfort, luxury, or creativity, but those spaces must also be livable and functional. Striking the right balance between **emotional desires** and **practical needs** is a critical skill for designers. A skilled designer, with strong sales abilities, can manage both aspects effectively when working with clients and their spaces. Failing to achieve this balance may result in either a dissatisfied client or losing the deal altogether.

Emotional vs. Practical Design:

- **Emotional Needs**: Clients may desire a space that feels **serene** or **luxurious**. Achieving this might involve soft color schemes, luxurious materials (like silk or velvet), or statement lighting that creates ambiance.

- **Practical Needs**: At the same time, the space must function well. A serene bedroom might also need **storage** for clothing and accessories, or the luxurious living room may need **durable furniture** if the client has children or pets.

5.6

Translating Client Desires into Concrete Design Concepts

Once the client's needs, preferences, and limitations are understood, the designer's role is to translate these insights into a coherent design concept. This involves synthesizing the functional and emotional elements into a visual and spatial solution. Clear communication and detailed presentations ensure the client aligns with the vision before moving forward with execution.

Steps to Translating Desires into Concepts:

- **Create Mood Boards**: Mood boards are an effective way to translate abstract client desires into concrete design ideas. They visually represent the color palettes, textures, furniture, and overall style of the proposed design.

- **Present Conceptual Sketches**: Provide **initial sketches** or **digital renderings** to show how their preferences will look in the actual space. Use software like **SketchUp** or **AutoCAD** to create visual representations.

- **Review and Refine**: Present these concepts to the client for feedback, encouraging them to voice their thoughts. Make refinements based on their input, ensuring that the final design reflects their vision and practical needs.

Key Point: Translating client desires into clear, visual design concepts helps bridge the gap between initial discussions and the actual implementation of the design.

Tool 5.7

Client Needs Assessment Worksheet

This worksheet helps interior designers gather and organize essential information about the client's needs, preferences, and constraints. The expanded sections allow for a deeper understanding of the client's lifestyle, functional requirements, and aesthetic preferences.

Client Needs Assessment Worksheet	
Client Name	________________________________
Contact Information	Email:_______________Phone:___________
Family Structure	Example: "Couple with two children (ages 5 and 7)"
Project Type	☐ Full Home Design ☐ Room Redesign ☐ Kitchen/Bath Renovation ☐ Other: __________
Property Information	
Location	Example: "Mumbai, 3BHK apartment in a high-rise building", "2 floor independent villa"
Approximate Are	Example: "1500 sq. ft.", "2500 sq. ft"
Existing Design Challenges	Example: "Poor lighting in the living room, lack of storage in the kitchen, feels cluttered"
Lifestyle Needs	
Daily Activities	Example: "Work from home two days a week, entertain guests frequently, children play area"
Special Requirements	Example: "Elderly parents living with us, need easy access to bathroom"
Preferred Ambiance/Feeling	Example: "We want the home to feel relaxing and spacious, but also elegant and contemporary"
Functional Needs	
Living Room	Example: "Comfortable seating for 8, space for TV and home theater system, easy-to-clean surfaces"
Kitchen	Example: "Ample countertop space, built-in storage for utensils and appliances, functional layout"
Master Bedroom	Example: "Walk-in closet, cozy but sophisticated, work-from-home corner"

Kids' Room	Example: "Durable furniture, study space, playful design, storage for toys and books"
Bathroom	Example: "Low-maintenance, modern fixtures, good ventilation, separate shower and tub"
Home Office	Example: "Quiet space with ergonomic furniture, large desk, plenty of storage"
Additional Rooms	Example: "Guest room with attached bathroom"
Aesthetic Preferences	
Overall Design Style	Example: ☐ Modern ☐ Contemporary ☐ Minimalist ☐ Traditional ☐ Eclectic ☐ Other:
Color Scheme	Example: "Neutral base with pops of color, prefer cool tones like blue and grey"
Materials Preferences	Example: "Sustainable materials like bamboo, natural wood, granite countertops, easy-to-maintain fabrics"
Lighting Preferences	Example: "Natural light where possible, ambient lighting for the living room, task lighting for the kitchen"
Texture and Finishes	Example: "Matte finishes, natural textures, prefer wood and stone over metal or glass"
Budget & Timeline	
Approximate Budget	☐ Below INR 5 Lac ☐ INR 5 -10 Lac ☐ INR 10 - 20 Lac ☐ Above INR 20 Lac
Priority Areas for Investment	Example: "Willing to invest in high-quality kitchen and living room furniture, flexible on other areas"
Budget Constraints	Example: "Must stay under INR 15,00,000, open to cost-effective alternatives for certain elements"
Preferred Timeline	Example: "Start in January, complete by June"
Key Decision Makers	Example: "Husband and wife making decisions together"
Preferred Communication Method	☐ Email ☐ Phone ☐ In-Person Meetings ☐ Other: _______________
Other Notes/Additional Requirements	Example: "Smart home integration, eco-friendly paint, Vastu-compliant layout"

Table 5.1 : Client Needs Assessment Worksheet

Tool 5.8

Wish List vs. Must-Haves Worksheet

This worksheet helps clients and designers prioritize features by separating the client's **"wish list"** (nice-to-have features) from **"must-haves"** (non-negotiable elements). It's a valuable tool to ensure that key functional and aesthetic elements are included while keeping the budget in check. More areas can be added as per project requirements.

Category	Wish List (Nice-to-Have Features)	Must-Haves (Essential Features)
Living Room	Designer furniture pieces (e.g., accent chairs, coffee table)	Comfortable seating for 8 people
	Decorative lighting like chandeliers or wall sconces	Ample storage space for media and books
	Artwork or gallery wall	Easy-to-clean flooring (e.g., hardwood or tile)
Kitchen	Premium finishes like marble countertops	Functional layout with efficient work triangle
	High-end appliances (e.g., built-in coffee machine, double-door fridge)	Durable countertops that can withstand heavy cooking
	Open shelving for display	Ample storage for pots, pans, and pantry items
Master Bedroom	Custom headboard and designer bedding	Spacious wardrobe or walk-in closet
	Feature wall with wallpaper or accent paint	Quiet, calming ambiance with blackout curtains
Kids' Room	Themed decor (e.g., superhero or princess design)	Durable, safe furniture (e.g., childproofed edges, low-height shelves)
	Custom-designed study nook	Sufficient storage for toys, books, and clothes
Bathroom	Spa-like features (e.g., rainfall shower, jacuzzi tub)	Good ventilation to avoid dampness

Table 5.2 : Wish List vs. Must-Haves Worksheet

Conclusion

The **client need analysis** process is an integral part of delivering successful interior design projects. By asking the right questions, probing deeper into unspoken desires, and balancing emotional needs with practical solutions, designers can create spaces that not only meet but exceed client expectations.

The use of structured tools such as the **Client Needs Assessment Worksheet** and **Wish List vs. Must-Haves Worksheet** further helps in organizing and translating client input into actionable design strategies, ensuring that the project runs smoothly and delivers optimal results.

6.

Analyzing and Prioritizing Client Needs

6.1 Prioritizing Needs by Space, Budget, and Timeline

6.2 Tools for Visualizing Client Needs (Mockups, Software)

6.3 Creating a Design Brief That Aligns with Client Goals

6.4 Common Pitfalls in Needs Analysis (Unrealistic Expectations)

6.5 Case Studies on Project Issues Needs Analysis

Tools & Formats:

6.6 Design Brief Template

6.7 Room Space Planning Template

6.0

Analyzing and Prioritizing Client Needs

Executive Summary

After conducting an in-depth client needs assessment and identifying functional and aesthetic preferences, the next step is analyzing those needs in a way that ensures they can be translated into practical, achievable design solutions. While clients often have a clear vision of their dream space, it is the interior designer's role to bridge the gap between aspirations and feasibility, balancing space, budget, and timeline limitations. Effective analysis of client needs allows the designer to align their creative solutions with realistic project constraints.

In this chapter, we will explore how designers can prioritize client needs, use tools for space visualization, and address common challenges that arise during the design process. A well-defined design brief serves as the foundation for aligning client expectations with what can practically be delivered, ensuring that the project runs smoothly and meets the client's goals.

6.1

Prioritizing Needs by Space, Budget, and Timeline

One of the key skills for any interior designer is the ability to **prioritize client needs** by considering the realities of space, budget, and timeline. Often, clients will present a broad range of desires, from luxurious finishes to high-end furniture, but not all elements may be feasible within the given constraints. The designer must determine which elements are essential and which can be adjusted, deferred, or replaced with more affordable alternatives.

Steps for Prioritizing Client Needs:

- **Assess Available Space**: The size and layout of the space often dictate which design features are realistic. For example, a client may want a large dining area with ample seating, but if the living space is limited, the designer might need to prioritize space-saving furniture or multifunctional pieces. In urban Indian cities like Mumbai and Delhi, where space is at a premium, this is particularly relevant. **Modular furniture** and **smart storage solutions** are key priorities in such cases.

- **Align with Budget**: A detailed discussion of the budget early on allows the designer to propose solutions that align with financial constraints. According to **Houzz's 2021 Renovation Survey**, about **50% of homeowners** in India experienced budget overruns due to a mismatch between their initial expectations and final costs. Prioritizing budget-critical elements such as structural work, key furniture pieces, and essential fixtures will help avoid these pitfalls.

- **Timeline Considerations**: Some design elements, such as custom furniture or imported materials, can significantly impact the project timeline. If a client has a tight deadline (e.g., moving into a new home), the designer may need to prioritize ready-made solutions or materials that are easily available. **Fast-track construction methods**, such as pre-fabricated components, can also be considered when the timeline is a major constraint.

Key Point: Prioritizing client needs based on space, budget, and timeline ensures that the project remains feasible and focused on the most important elements while managing client expectations effectively.

6.2

Tools for Visualizing Client Needs:

Mockups, Software

Visualization tools are invaluable for analyzing client needs and helping both the designer and client understand how design concepts will work within the actual space. By using software and mockups, designers can create **accurate representations** of the space, allowing clients to see how their needs will translate into reality.

Key Tools for Space Visualization:

- **3D Modeling Software**:

  - Tools like **SketchUp**, **AutoCAD**, and **Revit** are widely used in the design industry to create detailed 3D models of rooms and buildings. These tools allow designers to input accurate measurements, apply textures, colors, and materials, and show clients how different elements will look in the final design.

  - **SketchUp** is particularly popular for its user-friendly interface and its ability to produce quick, professional-looking 3D models that can be shared with clients.

- **Room Layout Planning Apps**:

  - Apps such as **RoomSketcher** and **Planner 5D** and many such other online tools offer clients and designers an easy way to visualize room layouts. These apps allow users to experiment with furniture placement, wall colors, and flooring to see how the space will be utilized.

  - In India, where many residential spaces have complex layouts (due to **Vastu Shastra** considerations or multi-generational living setups), such tools can help designers and clients explore multiple configurations quickly.

- **Virtual Reality (VR) and Augmented Reality (AR)**:

  - **Virtual Reality** technology is becoming more popular in high-end design firms for giving clients an immersive experience of their future space. Designers can create a virtual walk-through of the proposed design, allowing clients to visualize the spatial relationships between different elements.

- o **Augmented Reality** tools like **IKEA Place** allow clients to use their smartphones to see how furniture will fit into their actual room by overlaying 3D models into their physical space.

Key Point: Visualization tools help bridge the gap between design concepts and reality, allowing clients to see how their needs and preferences will be reflected in the final space. These tools also provide an effective way to **test out different design options** without committing to costly materials or layouts.

6.3

Creating a Design Brief:

Aligning Client Expectations with Practicalities

A **design brief** is a formal document that outlines the client's needs, goals, budget, timeline, and the agreed-upon design strategy. It serves as the blueprint for the entire project and ensures that both the client and designer are aligned on what the final outcome will be. The design brief is crucial for setting expectations and preventing miscommunication during the project.

Key Components of a Design Brief:

- **Project Overview**: A summary of the client's vision, including key functional and aesthetic goals.

  - o Example: "The client envisions a modern, minimalist home with a focus on natural materials and a neutral color palette. Key priorities include maximizing natural light and integrating smart home technology."

  - o Example: "The client desires a cozy, contemporary apartment that blends comfort with style. Key priorities include creating an open-concept living space, incorporating bold accent colors, and optimizing storage solutions while maintaining a warm, inviting atmosphere."

- **Client Needs and Preferences**: A breakdown of specific requirements for each room, including functional needs.

  - o Example: "Ample storage in the kitchen" and aesthetic preferences (e.g., "luxury finishes in the master bathroom".

- o Example: "A spacious and organized home office with a large desk area and built-in shelving for books and supplies. Aesthetic preference includes clean lines, neutral tones, and a calming atmosphere."

- o Example: "A comfortable and cozy living room with plenty of seating for entertaining. The client prefers a mix of modern and vintage furniture, with warm, earthy colors and soft textures for a welcoming vibe."

- **Budget and Timeline**:

  - o A detailed overview of the available budget and a breakdown of cost estimates for different areas. The timeline section should include key project milestones, such as **design approval, construction start date, and expected project completion**.

  - o Example: "The client has allocated a budget of $250,000 for the project. The budget should cover all design, construction, and material costs, with a focus on high-quality, sustainable finishes. Key milestones include design approval within the next 4 weeks, construction start in 8 weeks, and project completion expected in 6 months."

- **Design Challenges**:

  - o Highlight any potential challenges, such as **space constraints, structural issues, or material sourcing**. This section should also offer proposed solutions for overcoming these challenges.

  - o Example: "The space is an open-plan living area with limited wall space, which could pose challenges for creating defined zones. To address this, movable partitions and multi-functional furniture will be incorporated to create flexibility without compromising the flow of the space."

Key Point: A well-crafted design brief ensures alignment between client expectations and practical realities, providing a clear roadmap for the project's success. It serves as a vital tool for avoiding misunderstandings and delivering a final result that meets both functional and aesthetic goals. At the end of this chapter, a template of a design brief is provided to help you understand and effectively follow the process which sets a strong foundation for your work.

o

6.4

Common Pitfalls in Needs Analysis (Unrealistic Expectations)

Despite thorough needs assessments and visualization tools, designers often encounter challenges during the design process, particularly when clients' **expectations exceed reality** or **preferences change** mid-project.

Common Challenges:

- **Unrealistic Budget Expectations**:
  - Clients may have ambitious goals but limited budgets, which can lead to disappointment if not managed early.
  - For example, a client may want high-end finishes and custom furniture but only have a mid-range budget. Designers should be proactive in discussing costs upfront and presenting **budget-friendly alternatives** that still meet the client's aesthetic goals.

- **Changing Preferences**:
  - It is common for clients to change their minds during the project. For example, a client who initially wanted a minimalist design might start leaning toward a more eclectic style as they see design options. This can lead to delays, cost increases, and potential frustration for both parties.
  - To mitigate this, designers can present a **range of design options** at the beginning and encourage clients to finalize their decisions before construction begins.

- **Space Limitations**:
  - Clients often have ideas that are difficult to implement due to space constraints. For example, a client may want a large kitchen island in a small apartment. In these cases, designers must manage expectations and suggest alternative solutions, such as **foldable or multifunctional furniture**.

Key Point: Addressing these challenges requires **clear communication**, **budget management**, and flexibility to adjust designs as necessary while keeping the project on track.

6.5

Case Studies on Project Issues Needs Analysis

Case studies offer valuable insights into how careful analysis of client needs can prevent significant challenges later in the project.

Case Study 1:

Budget Overruns Avoided Through Proper Prioritization

- **Context**: A family in Bangalore wanted to renovate their 2BHK apartment with a limited budget of INR 12,00,000. They requested high-end materials, a custom kitchen, and designer furniture.
- **Solution**: The designer conducted a detailed needs analysis and explained that custom furniture would stretch the budget too far. By prioritizing **durable yet affordable materials and hardware** in the kitchen and recommending **ready-made furniture with warranty and** with a similar aesthetic, the designer was able to keep the project within budget.
- **Outcome**: The project was completed within budget and on time, with the client happy with the balance of quality and cost-efficiency.

Case Study 2:

Managing Changing Preferences with Flexibility

- **Context**: A luxury client in Mumbai initially requested a minimalist design but later decided they wanted a more eclectic, colorful space after seeing design mockups.
- **Solution**: The designer had already sensed the variable preferences during need analysis and created multiple design concepts during the planning stage, allowing the client to explore different options. By having pre-prepared alternatives, the designer was able to accommodate the client's changing preferences without delaying the project.
- **Outcome**: The project was completed successfully, with the client satisfied with the final eclectic design.

Key Point: Careful needs analysis helps identify potential challenges early, enabling designers to manage client expectations and project constraints effectively. By prioritizing key elements and maintaining flexibility, designers can avoid issues like budget overruns and design changes. Thoughtful planning leads to successful project outcomes.

Tool 6.6

Design Brief Template

Here is the template for the design brief that a designer should prepare for each project.

Interior Design Brief

P&G Interiors
24, Sky Marina, Udaipur - 313001
pg interior@pg.com, +91-9988776655

Project Name	Villa Waadi
Client Name	Myra & John
Due Date	6 Feb 2026
Total Budget	87 Lac

Project Overview:

The clients envision a modern, minimalist home with a focus on natural materials and a neutral color palette. Key priorities include maximizing natural light and integrating smart home technology. The project will involve transforming their existing 3-bedroom house into a contemporary space that aligns with their lifestyle needs and personal tastes.

Project Objective:

To design a functional, stylish, and sustainable living environment.
To create open and fluid spaces with seamless transitions between rooms.
To incorporate smart home features for increased convenience and energy efficiency and to maintain a balance between aesthetic appeal and practicality for everyday living.

User Persona:

The primary use for this design is Myra & John, a professional couple in their early 30s, who value both aesthetics and functionality. They prefer modern design, natural materials, and an eco-friendly approach using natural wood, stone, and glass to create a sophisticated, yet warm and inviting environment using whites, soft grays, and earthy tones.

---

cont..

Final Design:

A spacious open-concept living area that connects the kitchen, dining, and living room seamlessly.
Smart home systems integrated into lighting, climate control, and security.
A functional kitchen with ample storage and high-end appliances.
A serene and luxurious master bedroom with a spa-like bathroom featuring modern fixtures and finishes.

Design Challenges:

Finding ways to enhance natural light in spaces with limited windows while maintaining privacy and a minimalist look.
Incorporating smart technology seamlessly into the design without disrupting the minimalist aesthetic or cluttering the space.

Designer Name: Hiya PG

Date & Place: 4, April 2025, Udaipur

Tool 6.7

Room Space Planning Template

A Room Space Planning Template serves as a valuable tool in visualizing space constraints and organizing design details for each room. By breaking down the design brief into individual room documents, each with key sections like room name, dimensions, functional needs, and design considerations, designers can clearly assess the available space and its limitations.

The inclusion of room dimensions helps to accurately map out furniture placement and circulation areas. Functional needs highlight specific requirements, such as storage, seating, or lighting, ensuring that every room meets the client's lifestyle and preferences. Design considerations, such as style, color palette, and material choices, ensure aesthetic goals are aligned with the room's function. This structured approach helps prevent design conflicts, provides clarity, and streamlines the decision-making process. Additionally, the template enables easy adjustments and refinements throughout the design process, making it easier to adapt to changing client needs or space limitations.

Tool 6.7

Room Space Planning Template

This template helps the designer visualize space constraints and map functional needs in a single snapshot. It also allows clients to view the overall plan on one page, making it easy to see and compare all the details at a glance.

Room	Dimensions	Functional Needs	Design Considerations
Living Room	15' x 12'	Seating for 6, space for TV unit, coffee table	Space-saving furniture, focus on natural light
Kitchen	10' x 8'	Efficient work triangle, plenty of storage, easy-to-clean surfaces	Modular kitchen units, durable countertops
Master Bedroom	12' x 12'	Wardrobe space, king-sized bed, cozy but modern ambiance	Minimalist furniture, soft color palette, blackout curtains
Bathroom	8' x 6'	Separate shower area, good ventilation, storage for toiletries	Durable, water-resistant materials, space-efficient layout

Table 6.1 : Room Space Planning Template

Visualisation :

Along with the template, a plan drawing showing the basic placement of furniture, fixtures, and available space can be included.

This will provide the customer with a clear understanding of both the layout and how the product will fit within the space.

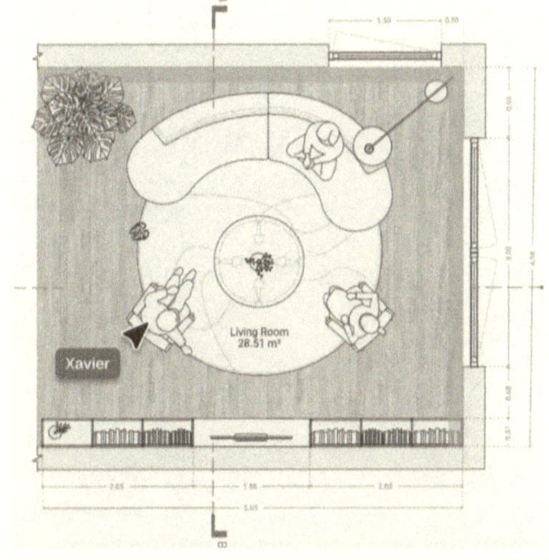

Conclusion:

Analyzing client needs effectively requires a careful balance of understanding the client's vision while managing the realities of space, budget, and timeline. By using visualization tools, creating detailed design briefs, and addressing common challenges, designers can ensure that their projects remain on track and aligned with client expectations. These strategies, supported by practical tools such as the **Design Brief Template** and **Room Layout Template**, provide a structured approach to delivering successful, client-focused design solutions.

7.

Matching Needs, Space & Budget Constraints

Tools & Formats:

Scan here
for more
digital
content

7.0

Matching Needs, Space & Budget Constraints

Executive Summary

Once the client's needs have been analyzed, the designer faces the critical task of aligning client expectations with the realities of space and budget. Residential interior design projects, especially in urban Indian contexts like Mumbai, Delhi, and Bangalore, often involve working with limited space and constrained budgets. The challenge lies in balancing these elements to create a design that fulfills the client's vision without compromising on quality, aesthetics, or functionality.

In this chapter, we will explore how designers can manage client expectations and optimize both space and budget while maintaining design integrity. Tools such as Value Engineering: Reducing Costs, Preserving Design help identify cost-effective alternatives without sacrificing quality. Design Engineering: Creative Compromise Solutions for Clients enables designers to find innovative ways to meet client needs through adaptable, functional design options. Additionally, Space Engineering: Optimizing Design and Budget focuses on maximizing space efficiency, ensuring that every square foot is used effectively within the client's financial constraints. These tools work together to offer comprehensive solutions that fulfill client demands while adhering to the project's limitations.

7.1

Managing Client Expectations: Educating Clients on Feasibility

One of the most critical aspects of a successful design project is ensuring that clients have a **realistic understanding of what can be achieved** within their budget and space constraints. In India, many residential clients, particularly first-time homeowners, may have high expectations influenced by **social media trends** or **luxury interior design magazines**, but may not fully understand the costs involved in achieving those designs.

Steps to Manage Expectations:

- **Educate Early**: During initial consultations, designers should provide clients with a clear breakdown of the costs involved for various design elements. This includes explaining the cost implications of luxury materials (e.g., marble, hardwood) versus more affordable alternatives (e.g., ceramic tiles, laminate).

  According to **Houzz's Renovation Survey** for India, **46% of homeowners** exceed their budgets, primarily due to a lack of understanding of material costs and scope expansion. Therefore, it's critical to inform clients about potential cost escalations.

- **Communicate Space Limitations**: In densely populated cities like Mumbai, where apartments are often small, it's important to help clients understand that **certain design elements** (e.g., large dining tables, expansive kitchen islands) may not be feasible. Offer space-saving alternatives such as **modular furniture** or **open-plan layouts** that maximize functionality within the available space.

- **Set Clear Priorities**: Guide clients in prioritizing their needs versus wants. For example, if the client has a limited budget but desires premium finishes, explain the trade-offs and suggest investing in high-impact areas (like the kitchen or living room) while using more cost-effective materials in less prominent spaces.

Key Point: Key Point: Effective expectation management requires transparency and education, ensuring that clients are informed and aligned with what is achievable within the given budget and space constraints. Regular updates and open communication throughout the design process will also help in preventing surprises and maintaining client satisfaction.

7.2

Presenting Budget, Mid-Range, and High-End Options

To help clients make informed decisions, designers should present a range of options that accommodate different **budget levels**. Offering **budget-friendly**, **mid-range**, and **high-end solutions** allows clients to visualize how their design choices impact both costs and aesthetics.

Breakdown of Design Options:

1. **Budget-Friendly Solutions**:

   - **Materials**: Laminate flooring, ceramic tiles, ready-made furniture, and prefabricated cabinetry.
   - **Design Elements**: Focus on maximizing functionality through **space-saving designs**, modular storage, and cost-effective finishes. For example, suggest **faux finishes** that mimic the appearance of luxury materials (e.g., faux wood or marble).
   - **Example**: A budget kitchen might feature **laminate countertops** and **standard-sized modular cabinets**, while still offering a sleek and modern aesthetic through thoughtful color and layout choices.

2. **Mid-Range Solutions**:

   - **Materials**: Engineered wood flooring, quartz countertops, semi-custom furniture, and upgraded appliances.
   - **Design Elements**: Balance quality with cost-efficiency. Focus on **durable materials** that offer long-term value. Mid-range designs often allow for **customization** in key areas (e.g., kitchen cabinetry or bathroom vanities) while keeping other areas more standardized.
   - **Example**: A mid-range living room may feature **engineered wood floors**, custom-built bookshelves, and **mid-tier fabric** for upholstery.

3. **High-End Solutions**:

   - **Materials**: Natural stone (marble, granite), hardwood flooring, custom-made furniture, and designer lighting.
   - **Design Elements**: High-end solutions focus on **luxury, craftsmanship, and exclusivity**. Every detail is tailored to the client's preferences using premium materials across the space.

- ○ **Example**: A luxury bathroom might feature **imported marble countertops**, custom vanities, high-end fixtures, and a **spa-like shower system**.

Key Point: Offering clients a range of options empowers them to choose the solution that best fits their budget while allowing them to visualize how their investment will impact the overall design. The designer's role is to present these options clearly, while guiding clients through the decision-making process to prevent confusion and overwhelm.

7.3

Space Engineering: Optimizing Design and Budget

Designing within constraints requires a combination of **creativity** and **strategic planning**. Even when working with limited budgets or small spaces, it's possible to achieve high-impact results through smart design choices. In India's urban landscape, maximizing every square foot of available space is essential, and designers often have to be resourceful in doing so.

Strategies for Maximizing Space and Budget:

1. **Multi-Functional Furniture**: In small apartments, furniture now days available are actually serves multiple purposes is a game-changer. For example, a **sofa bed** in the living room can double as a guest bed, or a **dining table with storage** can save space. Multi-functional furniture is widely used in **compact urban homes** and is becoming more available through online platforms like **Pepperfry** and **Urban Ladder**.

2. **Modular Design**: Modular systems for kitchens and wardrobes allow for flexibility while reducing costs. Modular units are easier to install and modify as needed, making them a great option for budget-conscious clients. According to **Livspace**, modular kitchens are up to **30% more affordable** than fully customized kitchens in India.

3. **Lighting and Mirrors**: Use **lighting** and **mirrors** strategically to create the illusion of a larger space. Well-placed lighting enhances the functionality of small spaces, while mirrors can reflect natural light, making rooms feel more open.

4. **Vertical Storage**: In compact homes, vertical space is often underutilized. Designers can maximize storage by incorporating **ceiling-high shelves**, **floating cabinets**, or even using **loft spaces** for additional storage.

Key Point: Even with tight constraints, designers can create impactful, functional designs by employing **space-saving techniques** and **cost-effective materials** without sacrificing quality.

7.4

Design Engineering: Creative Compromise Solutions

Designers must often find **creative ways to compromise** without making the client feel as though they are sacrificing their vision. By presenting alternatives that maintain both aesthetics and functionality, designers can offer solutions that meet client needs while staying within the project's limits.

Creative Compromise Strategies:

1. **Mixing High and Low-End Elements**: In many successful interior designs, luxury items are balanced with more affordable elements. For instance, a client may want **high-end Italian marble flooring**, but due to budget constraints, the designer could propose using **marble-look porcelain tiles** for areas like the hallway and entry, while reserving the real marble for focal areas like the bathroom or fireplace.

2. **Repurposing Existing Furniture**: Instead of purchasing all new furniture, suggest **repurposing or reupholstering** existing pieces to fit the new design scheme. This not only saves money but also allows the client to retain personal, meaningful items.

3. **Cost-Effective Decor**: Use **cost-effective decor** to enhance the space. For example, **paint** or **wallpaper** can dramatically change the feel of a room without a significant financial investment. Clients often appreciate these creative, low-cost solutions that still achieve the desired look.

Key Point: Finding creative compromises ensures that the client still feels they are receiving a high-quality design, even when certain elements must be adjusted to meet budget or space limitations.

7.5

Value Engineering: Cut Cost, Not The Design

Value engineering is a strategic approach focused on reducing project costs without compromising the quality, functionality, or aesthetic appeal of the design. In interior design, this process involves carefully assessing each aspect of the project—such as materials, methods, and products—and identifying alternatives that achieve similar results at a lower cost. By prioritizing efficiency and cost-effectiveness, designers can align with the client's vision while staying within budget.

Steps for Value Engineering:

- **Evaluate Core Material Substitutions:** One key area for value engineering is core material substitutions. For example, using **MDF** or **Plywood** instead of solid wood for furniture and cabinetry can maintain structural integrity and aesthetics while being significantly more affordable. These engineered materials offer durability and can be finished to mimic the appearance of solid wood.

- **Evaluate Finish Material Substitutions:** Another area to consider is the finish material. Using **premium laminate** finishes instead of **veneer** can achieve a similar look and texture, offering an attractive and cost-effective alternative for furniture surfaces or doors.

- **Evaluate Hardware Substitutions:** Hardware choices can also significantly impact costs. For instance, instead of offering extra drawers or additional hardware, evaluate whether all the proposed features are necessary. Replacing **sliding doors** with **swing doors**, for example, can reduce costs while still fulfilling functional needs, as sliding doors often require more complex hardware.

- **Local Sourcing**: In India, sourcing materials and furniture from **local artisans** or **manufacturers** can significantly reduce costs compared to imported products. This also supports the local economy and can add unique, handcrafted elements to the design.

Key Point: Value engineering allows designers to optimize budgets by evaluating core material substitutions, finish material options, hardware choices, and simplifying design elements, all while maintaining the integrity and aesthetic appeal of the original design. Through these adjustments, designers can deliver high-quality spaces within financial constraints.

Tool 7.6

Space Wise Budget Planning Worksheet

The Space vs Budget Planning Worksheet is a tool designed to help designers and clients align space requirements with budget constraints at macro level, ensuring optimal use of both. It provides a structured approach to balance functionality, aesthetics, and cost, facilitating smarter design decisions.

Option 1: Using standard specifications as per client requirements:

Room	Sq.ft	Estimated Cost	Recommended Solutions
Living Room	250	INR 2,50,000	Leather sofa, base mounted TV unit, and wall unit with shelving.
Kitchen	150	INR 3,00,000	Modular kitchen with drawers, quartz countertops, pull-out pantry, appliances
Master Bedroom	200	INR 2,00,000	Custom wardrobe, solid wood desk for work-from-home setup
Bathroom	100	INR 1,50,000	Hi-end fixtures, wall-mounted storage, Premium shower cubicle
Total Area	**700**	**INR 9,00,000**	

Option 2: Optimised to approx 15% reduction in cost using design and value engineering tools discussed earlier in case client expect alternative in space and budget while maintaining design integrity.

Room	Area	Estimated Cost	Recommended Solutions
Living Room	250	INR 1,70,000	Fabric sofa, wall-mounted TV unit, minimalist shelving
Kitchen	150	INR 2,10,000	Modular kitchen with drawers & shelves, granite countertops
Master Bedroom	200	INR 1,40,000	Modular wardrobe, foldable desk for work-from-home setup
Bathroom	100	INR 1,05,000	Premium fixtures, wall-mounted storage, compact shower cubicle
Total Area	**700**	**INR 7,30,000**	

Table 7.1 : Space Wise Budget Planning Worksheet

Conclusion

Balancing space, budget, and design demands requires careful analysis, creativity, and effective client communication. By presenting a range of options, employing value engineering, and finding innovative solutions that don't feel like sacrifices, designers can ensure that projects remain feasible and deliver satisfying results. Using tools such as the **Space Wise Budget Comparison Worksheet**, designers can offer clear, transparent solutions that meet both client expectations and project constraints.

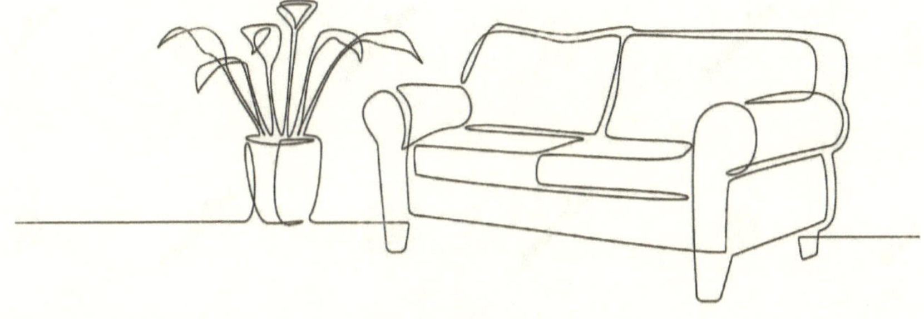

8.

Design Solutions Selling and Closing Deals

8.1 The Psychology of Selling Design Solutions

8.2 Structuring Design Presentations for Maximum Impact

8.3 Selling Value: Features vs. Benefits in Design

8.4 Overcoming Price, Timing, and Design Objections

8.5 Powerful Visual Aids: Renderings, Samples, and Models

8.6 Moving From Concept to Contract: Closing the Deal

Tools & Formats:

8.7 Design Presentation Workflow

8.8 Objection Handling Guide,

Scan here for more digital content

8.0

Design Solutions Selling and Closing Deals

Executive Summary

After conducting a thorough analysis of the client's needs and delivering viable solutions, the next step for interior designers is the presentation and sale of the final design concept. This process, often referred to as solution selling, focuses on presenting the design in a way that highlights its value to the client. Solution selling is distinct because it involves positioning the design as the answer to the client's specific needs, both functional and emotional, rather than focusing solely on aesthetics or individual features.

This chapter will explore the psychology behind why clients choose to buy based on value, how to structure impactful presentations, and how to handle objections effectively. It will also cover the role of visual aids in selling design concepts and the steps necessary to move from concept presentation to final contract.

8.1

The Psychology of Selling Design Solutions

Solution selling is rooted in the idea that clients buy a design not simply for what it looks like, but for the **value it provides** in solving their problems or enhancing their lifestyle. According to **research by Bain & Company**, **80% of customers** base their purchasing decisions on **perceived value**, rather than just cost or aesthetic appeal.

Key Psychological Drivers in Solution Selling:

- **Emotional Value**: Residential interior design is often a deeply personal experience for clients, as their homes reflect their identity and lifestyle. Designers should emphasize how the proposed design will make the client **feel**—whether it's comfort, luxury, or creativity. In India, emotions tied to **family well-being** and **cultural practices** (e.g., Vastu Shastra) can significantly influence design decisions. For instance, a family home designed for multi-generational living must emphasize practicality and comfort, which offers emotional reassurance to the client.

- **Functional Value**: Clients are not only seeking visually appealing spaces, but also functional ones that make their daily **lives easier.** Emphasizing how the design addresses common pain points, such as maximizing storage, improving lighting, or optimizing space usage. According to a report by **Livspace, 62%** of homeowners in India prioritize functionality over aesthetics when designing their homes, underscoring the importance of creating spaces that work seamlessly for their needs.

- **Financial Value**: Many well educated clients are sensitive to **long-term cost implications**, such as energy savings from sustainable materials or the return on investment (ROI) from a well-designed property. Solution selling should emphasize how the design can save money or increase the property's value over time. According to **Knight Frank India**, properties with well-designed interiors can appreciate by as much as **20%**, depending on the location and market conditions.

Key Point: Clients are motivated by the **value the design brings** to their life, whether it's emotional, functional, or financial. Understanding these drivers allows designers to tailor their presentation accordingly.

8.2

Structuring Your Design Presentation for Maximum Impact

An effective design presentation is **well-structured** and flows logically, helping the client understand both the concept and how it solves their needs. A carefully planned presentation allows the designer to maintain control of the discussion and guide the client through the decision-making process.

Steps to Structure a Design Presentation:

- **Introduction and Recap**: Begin by briefly recapping the **client's needs and objectives** as discussed in previous meetings. This reinforces that the designer understands the client's vision and has tailored the solution accordingly.

  - **Example**: "As we discussed, your main priorities for the living room were maximizing natural light, creating a cozy space for family gatherings, and incorporating a modern aesthetic."

- **Present the Concept**: Use **visual aids** (renderings, mood boards, and 3D models) to present the overall design. Focus on the key areas of the home and explain how the design addresses the client's functional, storage and aesthetic needs. It's essential to explain the **rationale** behind key decisions, such as material selection or layout changes.

  - **International Reference**: Designers like **Kelly Hoppen** emphasize the importance of visual storytelling in presentations, where each element is tied to a specific client need.

- **Breakdown of Features and Benefits**: Explain the **features of the design** and connect them to **specific benefits** for the client. (More detailed explanation is given in next subchapter number 8.3).

  - **Example**: "The modular storage system we've chosen not only saves space but also ensures that the room remains clutter-free, making it easier to maintain."

- **Cost-Benefit Analysis**: Present a **cost breakdown** for the project, highlighting where investments are being made and how they align with the client's priorities. This show's that you've considered the **financial aspect** of the design and, provided value-based options.

Call to Action: Conclude with a clear **call to action**, such as moving forward with the design or finalizing decisions on specific elements.

Key Point: A well-structured presentation highlights how the design solves client problems, showcases the value of each element, and guides the client toward a decision.

8.3

Selling Value: Features vs. Benefits in Design

One of the most critical elements of solution selling is the distinction between **features** and **benefits**. While **features** refer to the specific characteristics of a design (e.g., high-quality materials, modern lighting), **benefits** are the outcomes or advantages these features provide to the client. Communicating the **benefits** is key to convincing clients that your design adds real value to their lives.

Same product with same **Features** can give different **Benefit** to different users. "A working couple may see Benefits in quick and hassle free installation but A lady with 5 members family may see benefits in more storage, durability, and warranty of the product."

How to Distinguish Features from Benefits:

- *Feature*: *"This custom-built kitchen island includes a quartz countertop and built-in storage."*

- *Benefit*: *"The quartz countertop is durable and low-maintenance, perfect for a busy family. The built-in storage keeps the kitchen organized, reducing clutter and making meal prep more efficient."*

- *Feature*: *"We've chosen energy-efficient lighting with smart features for your home"*

- *Benefit*: *"Not only does it help reduce electricity bills, but it also contributes to creating a more sustainable, eco-friendly living environment. So, you'll feel good about saving on costs and minimizing your environmental footprint."*

Key Point: Always link the **features** of your design to the **specific benefits** they provide for the client. This reinforces the value of your solution and makes it more compelling.

8.4

Overcoming Price, Timing, and Design Objections

Even the best design presentations are likely to face objections. These can range from concerns about price and timeline to hesitations over design elements. Anticipating and addressing objections proactively is key to moving the project forward.

Common Objections and How to Handle Them:

1. **Price Objections**:

   - **Client**: "This design is more expensive than I anticipated."

   - **Response**: Acknowledge the concern and present a **cost-benefit analysis**. Emphasize long-term value, durability, and potential savings (e.g., "Investing in quality materials now will save you from costly repairs or replacements in the future."). Offer **alternative solutions** that maintain design integrity but reduce costs.

2. **Timeline Objections**:

   - **Client**: "Will this project take too long? I need the house ready by a certain date."

   - **Response**: Reassure the client by presenting a clear **project timeline** with milestones. Offer **solutions** to accelerate certain phases (e.g., "We can use pre-fabricated components in the kitchen to save time without compromising quality.").

3. **Design Hesitations**:

   - **Client**: "I'm not sure about the color scheme you've chosen."

   - **Response**: Offer to explore **alternative design options** or suggest doing a **mockup** of the space with different colors. Remind the client that flexibility in design is possible without losing the overall aesthetic.

Tool: At the end of this chapter, an Objection Handling Guide in table format is attached for your reference.

Key Point: Handling objections effectively involves **listening to the client's concerns** and offering solutions that make them feel confident in moving forward.

8.5

Powerful Visual Aids: Renderings, Samples, and Models

In the world of interior design, **visual communication** is crucial. Clients may not always be able to visualize a space from a verbal explanation or written description, so using **3D renderings, material samples, and models** can make the design concept more tangible and relatable. According to **Interior Design Magazine**, projects with detailed visual presentations are **30% more likely to close successfully** because clients feel more connected to the proposed design.

Types of Visual Aids:

1. **3D Renderings and Floor Plans**:

   - Using software like **AutoCAD**, **SketchUp**, or **Revit**, designers can create detailed renderings that show the client exactly how the space will look and function. Renderings allow for the exploration of different layout options, materials, and color schemes.

2. **Mood Boards**:

   - A mood board visually represents the **color palette, textures, and finishes** that will be used in the design. This is especially effective for showing the client how different elements will come together to create a cohesive look.

3. **Material Samples**:

   - Providing physical samples of materials (e.g., fabric swatches, tiles, wood) allows clients to experience the **tactile qualities** of the design. This helps them feel more confident in the quality and appropriateness of the materials.

4. **Models**:

   - Physical or **3D-printed models** can be used to show the client the spatial arrangement of furniture, walls, and key features. These are particularly useful for more complex or custom-built projects.

Key Point: Visual aids are essential in helping clients visualize and emotionally connect with the design. The more real the concept feels, the easier it is for the client to make a decision.

8.6

Moving From Concept to Contract: Closing the Deal

After presenting the design concept and addressing any objections, the final step is **closing the sale** and formalizing the agreement. This involves gaining the client's approval on the design and moving forward with the contract.

Steps to Close the Sale:

1. **Recap and Confirm Agreement**: Summarize the agreed-upon design elements, budget, and timeline to ensure that there is **no ambiguity**. Ask the client if they have any final questions or concerns.

2. **Present the Contract**: Provide a clear, detailed contract that outlines the **scope of work**, project timeline, payment schedule, and any contingencies for changes. Make sure the contract reflects all the agreed terms.

3. **Call to Action**: Encourage the client to **sign the contract** and move forward with the project. Offer to address any final hesitations they might have.

Example:

- "I'm confident this design meets all of your needs, and with your approval today, we can begin the implementation phase by the end of the week."

- "By signing today and providing the advance, we can lock in an extra 5% discount on materials, as it's the closing week of the month. This will help you to save a considerable amount while getting the project started on time."

- "If we finalize the contract and deposit today, I can secure an additional one-year warranty on the cabinetry and additional 10% discount on all kitchen appliances, as part of our month-end promotion. This ensures both value and long-term security for your investment."

Key Point: Closing the sale effectively involves recapping the agreed terms, presenting a clear contract, and providing a compelling call to action. Offering timely incentives can help motivate clients to commit and move forward with the project.

Tool 8.7

Design Presentation Workflow

Here's an example of a Design Presentation Workflow in tabular form to guide your start to end presentation process:

Sn	Section	Detailed Worksheet, Decks & Documents
1	Introduction	Brief introduction of the design team and company. Overview of the project's objectives and the client's needs.
2	Design Concept Overview	Present the visual renderings, mood boards, and floor plans, explaining how each element aligns with the client's needs and vision.
3	Floor Plans & Layouts	Detailed floor plans and layout options, explaining spatial configurations and how the layout enhances functionality and flow.
4	Material Selections	Showcase material choices (e.g., fabrics, finishes, countertops), connecting these selections to both aesthetic goals and practical benefits (e.g., durability).
5	Color Palette & Theme	Presentation of the chosen color scheme and theme, explaining how they unify the space while fitting the client's preferences.
6	3D Views & Renderings	Provide 3D mockups and renderings to give the client a realistic preview of the proposed design.
7	Budget Breakdown	Provide a detailed breakdown of the costs, covering materials, labor, and any additional fees, and explain how the budget was allocated to maximize value.
8	Timeline & Milestones	Present a project timeline with clear milestones (e.g., design approval, procurement, construction), ensuring realistic delivery within the agreed timeframe.
9	Objections Addressed	Address any concerns the client raised during the consultation process, explaining how adjustments were made (e.g., cost reductions, alternate materials).
10	Next Steps/Closing	Summarize the action items and remaining decisions. Encourage the client to approve the design, sign the contract, and confirm the advance payment.

Table 8.1 : Design Presentation Workflow

Tool 8.8

Objection Handling Guide

This table provides common objections raised by clients during the design process, along with realistic responses and suggested solutions. These can help designers navigate conversations about budget, design preferences, timing, and other concerns.

Objection	Client Concern	Suggested Response	Proposed Solution
Too Expensive	*This design is more than I planned to spend.*	I understand your concern. Let's review the cost breakdown together and identify areas where we can adjust without losing the overall impact of the design.	Offer to replace high-cost items (e.g., using laminate instead of natural wood or porcelain tiles instead of marble) to reduce costs without sacrificing quality.
Tight Timeline	*I need the project finished earlier than planned.*	I can work with the contractors to prioritize the critical phases and streamline some of the decisions so we can move quickly.	Fast-track certain components, such as using prefabricated cabinetry, or working with readily available materials to speed up delivery.
Uncertain About Design Choice	*I'm not sure if this layout will work for my lifestyle.*	We can explore alternative layouts and make adjustments to better suit your routine. Would you like to see other options for how to maximize the space?	Offer a 3D rendering or alternate layout options to give a clearer visual of how the space could function, using flexible layouts that fit their daily activities.
Concern About Maintenance	*I'm worried about the these materials. Will they be easy to maintain?*	The materials I've selected are durable and require minimal maintenance. Let me walk you through how to keep them looking great for years to come.	Suggest low-maintenance materials, like quartz countertops instead of marble, or recommend fabrics with easy-clean finishes for furniture.

Objection	Client Concern	Suggested Response	Proposed Solution
Color/Style Uncertainty	*I don't know if this color scheme will work for me. I like more neutral.*	We can adjust the palette to something you feel more comfortable with. Let's look at a few alternatives that still work with the overall design concept.	Offer alternative color schemes and suggest a mockup with different options to help the client visualize their preferences in the context of the full design.
Not very comfortable with Custom Solutions	*What if I don't like the custom furniture once it's built?*	I understand your concern. We can explore semi-custom or modular pieces that offer flexibility while still providing a tailored look.	Provide examples of semi-custom furniture options from manufacturers that allow customization of specific elements with flexibility.
Worried About ROI (Return on Investment)	*Will this renovation increase my home's value? Is this a smart investment?*	Investing in key areas like kitchens and bathrooms and durable material will certainly improve the value.	Features like energy-efficient systems, quality materials in high-traffic areas, and timeless design choices that increase resale value.
Environment al Concerns	*I want eco-friendly materials, but they seem expensive.*	Let's look at alternatives that offer eco-friendliness without significantly increasing costs.	Recommend sustainable options like bamboo, recycled wood, and low-VOC paints, widely available in the Indian market.
Worried About Disruption to Daily Life	*I'm worried about how the renovation will affect my family's routine.*	We can plan the work in phases to minimize disruption. I'll work with the contractors to ensure critical areas remain usable as much as possible.	Phase the renovation so that important areas (like the kitchen or bathroom) are done quickly or during vacation periods to minimize inconvenience.

Table 8.2 : Objection Handling Guide

Conclusion

Solution selling in interior design goes beyond presenting a visually appealing space—it involves demonstrating how the design **solves the client's problems**, enhances their lifestyle, and adds long-term value. By understanding the psychology of solution selling, structuring presentations effectively, and handling objections with confidence, designers can build trust with clients and close deals more effectively. With tools such as the **Design Presentation Template** & **Objection Handling Guide**, designers can navigate the final stages of the sales process smoothly, moving from concept to contract and ensuring successful project outcomes.

9.

Managing Client Relationships During Design

9.1 Effective Communication of Project Progress

9.2 Managing Changes and Avoiding Scope Creep

9.3 Setting Realistic Timelines and Milestones

9.4 Handling Delays, Vendor Issues, and Other Challenges

9.5 Keeping Clients Satisfied Without Overpromising

9.6 Building Client Loyalty for Future Projects

Tools & Formats:

9.7 Project Timeline Planogram

9.8 Scope Change Request Form

Scan here for more digital content

9.0

Managing Client Relationships During Design

Executive Summary

Effective client relationship management is critical during the design phase of any project. The design phase is where ideas come to life, but it's also where challenges such as delays, revisions, and scope creep can occur. Successfully managing the client relationship involves clear and consistent communication, setting realistic expectations, and addressing concerns before they escalate. Maintaining transparency and being proactive during this phase can strengthen trust and help turn a one-time project into a long-term partnership.

This chapter explores the best practices for managing client relationships during the design phase, handling challenges like scope creep and delays, and ensuring client satisfaction throughout the project. We will also introduce key tools such as a Project Timeline Template, Scope Change Request Form, and Client Progress Report Template to help structure these processes.

9.1

Effective Communication of Project Progress

Clear, consistent communication keeps clients engaged and informed throughout the design phase. Poor communication can lead to misunderstandings, delays, or unmet expectations. Effective communication reassures clients that the project is on track and encourages feedback before key decisions are made.

Best Practices for Communicating Progress:

- **Scheduled Updates**: Set up regular check-ins (weekly or bi-weekly) with the client to review the project's status. These updates can be through **in-person meetings**, **emails**, or **video calls**, depending on the client's preferences. Scheduled Updates are more conversational and frequent, designed to maintain ongoing dialogue and provide immediate feedback.

  - **Data from the Harvard Business Review** suggests that regular communication reduces client dissatisfaction and **increases project success rates by 40%**.

- **Client Progress Reports**: Use **progress reports** to summarize what has been completed, what is in progress, and what's upcoming. These reports help everyone in team to ensure transparency and provide a written record of the project's status. Client Progress Reports are formal, structured summaries of the project's progress, offering an overview of the work done, and often used for documenting milestones.

  - **Indian Context**: In India, where personal rapport often plays a key role in business relationships, designers should balance **formal reports with personal communication** to build a strong connection.

- **Visual Aids**: Sharing **visual updates** such as **3D renderings**, mood boards, or even photos of on-site work can help clients visualize progress and stay excited about the project.

Key Point: Consistent and transparent communication, including regular updates and visual aids, helps keep clients informed and engaged throughout the project. This approach fosters trust, reduces dissatisfaction, and enhances project success.

9.2

Managing Changes and Avoiding Scope Creep

Scope creep occurs when a project expands beyond its original boundaries, often without an increase in budget or timeline. It can cause delays, cost overruns, and client dissatisfaction. To avoid this, designers must manage changes and revisions effectively.

How to Handle Scope Creep?:

- **Clear Scope Definition**: At the outset, ensure the project scope is well-defined and agreed upon in the contract. Include specific **deliverables, timelines, and costs**. If the client requests additional work, refer back to the initial scope.

  - **International Reference**: According to **PMI's 2021 Pulse of the Profession**, nearly **52% of projects** experience scope creep, primarily due to unclear scope at the start.

- **Change Request Process**: Establish a formal **scope change request process**. When clients request changes, have them complete a **Scope Change Request Form** that details the change, the reasons for it, and the impact on **budget and timeline**. This ensures both parties agree on how to handle the change.

- **Communicate the Impact**: Be clear about how any changes will affect the overall project. For example, if the client requests a change in materials, explain how that will alter the timeline, labor requirements, and final cost.

Key Point:Key Point: Effectively managing scope creep involves clearly defining the project scope upfront, using a formal change request process, and communicating the impact of any changes on budget and timeline.

9.3

Setting Realistic Timelines and Milestones

Setting clear expectations around timelines and milestones ensures that the client understands when to expect key deliverables and what progress will look like at each stage. **Realistic timelines** reduce frustration and help prevent unnecessary revisions.

Strategies for Managing Timelines:

1. **Detailed Project Timeline**: Provide a **project timeline** at the start, broken down by phases (e.g., design, procurement, construction). This should include major **milestones**, such as when the client can expect to approve design concepts, material selections, and the final walkthrough.

   - **Example of Phases**:
     - Conceptual Design: 3 Weeks
     - Design Approval: 1 Week
     - Material Selection: 2 Weeks
     - Installation and Construction: 8 Weeks

2. **Set Buffer Time**: Include a buffer for potential delays, such as material delivery issues or unforeseen site conditions. **India's monsoon season**, for instance, may cause delays in construction projects, particularly in cities like Mumbai.

3. **Communicate Delays Proactively**: If delays occur, inform the client as soon as possible and explain the reasons. Clients are more understanding if they are kept informed rather than surprised at the last minute. In the **UK**, according to the **RIBA Plan of Work**, client satisfaction increases when designers communicate changes to timelines clearly and provide updated schedules.

Key Point: Setting a detailed project timeline with clear milestones, including buffer time for potential delays, ensures that clients have realistic expectations. Proactively communicating any changes to the schedule enhances client satisfaction. Clear communication reduces misunderstandings and improves overall project success.

9.4

Handling Delays, Vendor Issues, and Other Challenges

Delays and issues with **vendors** or **contractors** are common challenges in interior design projects. How these issues are handled can determine the client's overall satisfaction with the project. Transparent communication and proactive solutions are essential to maintaining trust and confidence throughout the project. Additionally, having backup vendors or contingency plans in place can help mitigate the impact of unforeseen challenges.

How to Handle Common Challenges:

1. **Vendor Delays**: If a supplier cannot deliver materials on time, immediately offer alternatives choice to the client. Present options that meet their **design and budget** requirements and explain any differences.

   ○ **Indian Reference**: Due to India's **dependence on imports** for certain luxury materials, supply chain disruptions can cause delays. Always have local alternatives available in case of international shipment delays.

2. **On-Site Challenges**: Construction or installation issues can arise, such as discovering that certain materials cannot be used as planned. Communicate the problem to the client quickly and provide **solution options**, including the timeline and cost impact.

3. **Project Revisions**: If revisions are required due to site conditions (e.g., unexpected structural issues), work with the client and contractor to **minimize disruptions**. Provide a clear **scope change form** that outlines how the revisions will affect the project.

Key Point: Proactive problem-solving and clear communication with clients are key to maintaining trust during challenges. Offering immediate solutions and alternatives ensures that the project stays on track despite delays or unforeseen issues.

9.5

Keeping Clients Satisfied Without Overpromising

Managing client expectations and maintaining satisfaction requires balancing excellent service with avoiding overpromising. Overpromising can result in disappointment if the final outcome doesn't meet expectations, especially concerning timelines, costs, or design features.

Best Practices for Keeping Clients Satisfied:

1. **Underpromise and Overdeliver**: Set realistic expectations about what is achievable within the scope, budget, and timeline, and then strive to **exceed** those expectations in key areas. For example, aim to finish before the agreed deadline or provide an unexpected value-add (e.g., upgraded fixtures).

2. **Be Transparent About Constraints**: If a client's vision exceeds their budget, be honest about what's possible and offer alternative options that fit within their means. Avoid agreeing to features that are outside the project's scope just to secure the client's approval. Clearly outline the cost implications of any upgrades so clients can make informed choices.

Key Point: Client satisfaction comes from delivering on promises and being **transparent** about budget, timeline, and design constraints and limitations.

9.6

Building Client Loyalty for Future Projects

Client loyalty is a valuable asset for any designer, as **repeat business** and **referrals** often stem from strong relationships built during the first project. Establishing a reputation for reliability, creativity, and trustworthiness can turn a one-time project into a long-term partnership.

Strategies for Building Long-Term Loyalty:

1. **Follow-Up After Project Completion**: Once the project is complete, follow up with the client to ensure they are satisfied with the results. Offer post-completion services such as **maintenance tips** or periodic checks to make sure everything remains in good condition.

2. **Referral Programs**: Encourage clients to refer friends and family by offering referral incentives, such as a **discount** on future services or a **gift** for successful referrals.

3. **Offer Additional Services**: Continue to engage clients by offering **seasonal updates**, maintenance packages, or smaller design consultations (e.g., for a room refresh or home office setup). This keeps the designer top-of-mind for future projects.

4. **Stay Connected**: Periodically update clients with **design trends** or news about your work via email or social media. This keeps the relationship alive and positions the designer as a trusted consultant for future projects.

Key Point: Long-term loyalty is built by going above and beyond during and after the project, maintaining relationships even after the final handover.

Tool 9.7

Project Timeline Planogram

A Project Timeline Planogram is a visual representation or chart that outlines the schedule and milestones of a project, typically used in design, construction, and other project-based industries. It combines elements of a project timeline (showing key deadlines, tasks, and deliverables) with the concept of a planogram to organize and display tasks in a clear, structured format.

PROJECT TIMELINE PLANOGRAM				
Task/Phase	**W1**	**W2**	**.. W14**	**Milestone**
Concept Design	•	•		Concept Finalized
- Client Consultation	•			First Client Meeting
- Draft Design		•		Design Proposal Ready
- Client Revisions & Approval		•		Design Approved
Material Selection				Materials Ordered
- Present Options & Finalize				Materials Chosen
- Orders Placed				Orders Confirmed
Construction Phase 1				Site Ready for Finishes
- Site Demolition				Old Structures Removed
- Plumbing & Electrical Rough-In				Rough Installation Complete
- Wall Framing & Drywall				Walls Ready
Construction Phase 2				Finishing Started
- Flooring Installation				Flooring Complete
- Cabinet & Fixture Installation				Fixtures Installed
- Final Painting & Finishes				Painting Complete
Final Walkthrough				Final Client Review
- Client Inspection				Client Walkthrough
- Punch List & Adjustments			•	Adjustments Made
Final Handover			•	Project Complete

Table 9.1 : Project Timeline Planogram

Explanation of the Planogram Timeline:

- **Parallel Tasks:** Many activities run simultaneously in a design project. For example, **concept design** can finish while **material selection** is being finalized, and construction phases can overlap, like plumbing and electrical rough-ins occurring alongside material selections.

- **Phases and Duration:** Each task is marked with **solid dots** (•) to show its start and duration. Parallel tasks span multiple weeks to streamline the project and minimize delays.

- **Milestones:** Key milestones are shown in the right column for easy tracking of **major deliverables** (e.g., concept approval, construction completion).

- **Critical Path:** Tasks like **flooring installation** can't start until **demolition** and **framing** are completed, showing activity dependencies

How to Use the Planogram Timeline?

- **Visual Scheduling:** Use this timeline to visually present the project schedule, showing overlapping tasks and highlighting critical paths to ensure smooth project flow.

- **Client Meetings:** Refer to this timeline during client meetings to update them on progress, delays, or changes in real-time.

- **Team Coordination:** The planogram helps synchronize schedules for contractors, designers, and suppliers, like planning material orders alongside construction to minimize delays.

Why This Timeline is Beneficial?

- **Clear Visual Representation**: This timeline visually communicates complex project details in a digestible format, making it easy for both clients and team members to follow.

- **Efficient Planning**: By showing **parallel activities**, this planogram helps avoid bottlenecks and enables simultaneous progress in different areas.

- **Transparency**: Clients are more likely to trust the designer when they are provided with a transparent view of what's happening at each stage of the project.

Tool 9.8

Scope Change Request Form

The **Scope Change Request Form** is used to manage any alterations to the original project scope. It helps ensure clear communication between the designer and client, detailing changes, their impact on the budget and timeline, and obtaining necessary approvals.

Scope Change Request Form				
Change Request	**Description of Change**	**Impact on Budget**	**Impact on Timeline**	**Reason for Change**
Flooring Change of Living Area	Change from laminate to hardwood flooring.	INR 80,000	Adds 2 weeks to material delivery time.	Client requested higher-end material.
Additional Shelving in Modular Kitchen Tall Unit	Request for additional custom shelving in the kitchen.	INR 25,000	No impact on timeline (prefabricate d shelving)	Client desires additional storage space.
Total Impact		**INR 1,05,000**		
Approval Process				
Requested By	**Reviewed By**	**Approval Status**	**Client Signature**	**Date of Signature**
Impact Summary				
Budget Impact	**Timeline Impact**	**Revised Budget**	**Revised Timeline**	**Client Signature**

Table 9.2 : Scope Change Request Form

Instructions: Complete all sections with relevant details for any requested changes to the scope of work. Attach supporting documentation (e.g., drawings, images, or revised designs) as needed. Submit this form to the client for review and sign-off on approval.

Conclusion

Managing the client relationship during the design phase requires **effective communication**, **proactive issue management**, and transparent handling of changes. By setting clear timelines and expectations, providing regular updates, and addressing any challenges swiftly, designers can maintain client satisfaction and build long-term loyalty. Using tools such as the **Project Timeline Template** and **Scope Change Request Form** helps structure the communication process and keeps the project on track, ensuring a smooth and successful outcome for both the client and the designer.

10.

Overseeing Site Execution and Final Delivery

10.1 Design to Construction Execution Transition

10.2 Coordinating with Contractors, Suppliers, and Installers

10.3 Ensuring Quality Control During Execution

10.4 Real-Time Problem Solving On-Site

10.5 Conducting the Final Client Walkthrough

10.6 Site Handover and Delivering Maintenance Plans

Tools & Formats:

10.7 Site Visit Checklist

10.8 Final Walkthrough Guide

Scan here
for more
digital
content

10.0

Overseeing Site Execution and Final Delivery

Executive Summary

Site execution is the culmination of the entire design process, where all conceptual and planning efforts translate into a tangible reality. This stage involves overseeing construction, ensuring quality, handling on-site challenges, and conducting the final handover. Successful site execution requires close coordination between the designer, contractors, suppliers, and clients to deliver a final product that aligns with the original design vision and client expectations.

This chapter explores how to manage the transition from design to construction, maintain quality control, handle real-time issues, and finalize the project with client walkthroughs and handover.

10.1

Design to Construction Execution Transition:

The transition from the design phase to construction is a critical juncture where the project moves from the **conceptual to the physical**. During this phase, it's essential to ensure that the design is properly communicated to contractors and installers, and that everyone understands the design intent.

Key Steps for Managing the Transition:

1. **Kickoff Meeting:** Before construction commences, a detailed kickoff meeting with contractors, suppliers, and stakeholders is crucial. This meeting should review the project's objectives, timelines, design specifics, and any particular requirements. This ensures that everyone involved is aligned with the design intent and construction strategy.

   - **Reference:** According to **The Architect's Handbook of Professional Practice (AIA, 2020)**, kickoff meetings are essential in setting clear expectations and fostering collaboration between the design and construction teams.

2. **Design Documentation**: Ensure that all necessary **design documentation** (including **3D renderings**, **blueprints**, and **specifications**) is handed off to the site team. Clarify any complex or custom features, such as unique joinery or bespoke installations.

3. **On-Site Presence**: During the initial stages of construction, the designer or project manager should have an **on-site presence** to confirm that the construction is being executed as per the design. This helps identify and correct any early-stage misalignments between the design and construction.

   - **Reference:** As detailed in **The Project Manager's Guide to Construction (Wiley, 2018)**, early-stage site visits are crucial to preventing design errors from being compounded during later stages of the project.

Key Point: A successful transition from design to construction hinges on clear communication, careful documentation, and ongoing oversight. Proper management at this stage helps ensure that the design vision is realized while minimizing errors and delays.

10.2

Coordinating with Contractors, Suppliers, and Installers:

How to Coordinate the Team?

Coordination is essential to ensure that the right materials and labor are available at the right time. A successful project relies on the designer's ability to work closely with contractors, suppliers, and installers, ensuring seamless execution.

Best Practices for Coordination:

1. **Detailed Schedule**: Provide a **detailed project schedule** that includes milestones for each phase of the construction process (e.g., framing, electrical work, painting). This ensures that suppliers and contractors are aware of their deadlines and that dependencies between tasks are clear.

   - **Reference:** As described in **The Architect's Handbook of Professional Practice (AIA, 2020)**, creating a project timeline with clearly defined phases is fundamental to coordinating the efforts of the design and construction teams. It helps avoid misunderstandings and streamlines the overall workflow.

2. **Clear Communication Channels**: Establish **clear communication channels** between the designer, contractors, and suppliers. Use tools like **WhatsApp** or **project management software** and tools like Asana or Trello, to ensure real-time updates on progress, deliveries, and issues.

   - **Reference: Project Management for Construction by Chris Hendrickson (Prentice Hall, 2009)** emphasizes the importance of real-time communication in managing construction projects, noting that the use of digital tools ensures better tracking and fewer communication gaps among project teams.

3. **Regular Site Meetings**: Hold **regular site meetings** (weekly or bi-weekly) to track progress, address concerns, and discuss any adjustments that may need to be made due to unforeseen site conditions.

Key Point: Effective coordination ensures that the right resources (materials and labor) are available at the right time, preventing delays and miscommunications.

10.3

Ensuring Quality Control During Execution

Maintaining quality control throughout the site execution phase is essential to ensure the final product aligns with the original design vision and meets the client's expectations. Quality issues may arise from poor workmanship, material substitutions, or deviations from the design. Deploying a skilled labor force on-site is crucial and plays a key role in the successful execution of the project. Here are a few important steps to follow:

Steps for Ensuring Quality Control:

1. **Site Visit Checklists**: Use a **Site Visit Checklist** during every on-site inspection. This checklist ensures that all critical elements, such as **finishes**, **fixtures**, and **structural elements**, are inspected and meet the required standards.

2. **Regular Inspections**: Conduct **regular inspections** at key stages of the interior process, such as after framing, electrical rough-in, and before the final finishes are applied. These inspections help identify any deviations from the plan early and prevent costly rework later.

   o **Indian Reference**: In India, quality control is often a challenge due to **labor skill gaps**. It's essential to work closely with trusted contractors and conduct more frequent inspections to maintain quality.

3. **Material Verification**: Check that materials delivered to the site match the **approved specifications**. If a substitution is needed due to availability, always inform the client and provide alternatives that match the original quality and design intent.

4. **Detailed Installation Guides**: Provide installers with **installation guides** for custom features, ensuring that complex installations (e.g., cabinetry, complex hardware, modular furniture or bespoke lighting) are executed to design specifications.

Key Point: Maintaining quality control during site execution ensures the final product meets design and client expectations. Regular inspections, material verification, and clear installation guidelines help prevent deviations. In regions like India, frequent checks and collaboration with skilled contractors are crucial for overcoming quality challenges.

10.4

Real-Time Problem Solving On-Site:

Handling On-Site Issues

On-site issues are inevitable in any construction project. These could include delays in material delivery, incorrect installations, or unexpected structural challenges. Quick problem-solving is essential to keep the project on track.

Problem-Solving Strategies:

- **Real-Time Decision-Making:** Ensure that a member of the design or project management team is always accessible to make swift, informed decisions on-site. This allows the team to address problems immediately, such as suggesting alternative materials or designs to replace unavailable items. In projects with high complexity, real-time decision-making can reduce downtime by up to 25%, as teams do not need to wait for external approval to move forward.

    - Example: If a specified tile becomes unavailable, the designer should immediately recommend an approved substitute to avoid any delays in construction.

- **On-Site Issue Logs**: Maintain a comprehensive issue log on-site, where contractors or supervisors can document every encountered problem, the solution implemented, and any adjustments made to the timeline or budget. This log provides a detailed record of issues, ensures accountability, and tracks the resolution process, allowing the team to address recurring issues proactively.

- **Client Communication**: If an issue requires client approval (such as a major change or additional costs), communicate clearly and present **solution options**. Always outline the potential impact on the timeline and budget. Projects that maintain continuous and clear communication with clients during problem-solving processes see a 15% improvement in client satisfaction and trust.

Key Point: Real-time problem-solving, swift decision-making, and transparent communication with both the team and the client are essential to mitigate on-site challenges. By maintaining an issue log and having backup solutions in place, construction projects can minimize delays and keep both the schedule and budget intact.

10.5

Conducting the Final Walkthrough with Clients:

Ensuring Satisfaction

The **final walkthrough** is a crucial moment where the designer presents the finished project to the client, ensuring that all elements are completed to their satisfaction. It is the last opportunity to identify any remaining issues before handover.

Steps for a Successful Final Walkthrough:

1. **Pre-Walkthrough Inspection**: Before the client arrives, conduct a **pre-walkthrough inspection** using a **Final Walkthrough Guide**. This ensures that everything is in place, and any last-minute adjustments can be made.

2. **Room-by-Room Inspection**: During the walkthrough, go through the project room by room, explaining key design features and answering any questions the client may have. This is also the time to take note of any **snag list** (punch list) items that require attention. According to **Interior Design Handbook by Joanna Wissinger,** the walkthrough is an essential step for providing the client with a clear understanding of the final product, allowing them to make informed decisions about any changes or adjustments needed.

3. **Collect Client Feedback**: Ensure the client is satisfied with the final result. Ask for **feedback** on the project and address any minor adjustments needed before formal handover.

4. **Document the Punch List**: If there are any remaining issues (such as touch-ups or missing items), document them in a **Punch List** and provide a timeline for their resolution. **The Architect's Handbook of Professional Practice** highlights that maintaining a Punch List is a best practice for ensuring that all outstanding tasks are completed before the final handover, preventing misunderstandings and ensuring client satisfaction.

Key Point: The final walkthrough is a critical opportunity to ensure the project meets client expectations. A structured approach, beginning with a pre-walkthrough inspection, followed by a detailed room-by-room review, collecting client feedback, and documenting the Punch List, ensures that any remaining issues are promptly addressed.

10.6

Site Handover and Delivering Maintenance Plans

The handover marks the formal conclusion of the project, where the client receives the final design along with all relevant documentation and maintenance guidelines.

Handover Process:

1. **Final Documentation**: Provide the client with **final documentation**, including:

   o **As-built Drawings:** Detailed drawings of the completed project, reflecting any changes made during construction and the final design specifications.

   o **Warranty Information:** Clear and organized warranty details for all materials, fixtures, and appliances, outlining the coverage periods and terms of service.

   o **Maintenance Instructions:** Specific care guidelines for all materials, finishes, and appliances used, ensuring the client knows how to properly maintain each element to preserve its longevity and appearance over time.

2. **Maintenance Plan**: Provide a detailed **maintenance plan**, particularly for high-end materials that require specific care (e.g., natural stone, hardwood floors). This helps ensure that the client maintains the design's quality over time.

3. **Client Training**: If the design includes **smart home systems** or specialized appliances, offer a **training session** for the client to familiarize them with the new technology.

4. **Post-Completion Check-In**: Schedule a **post-completion check-in** (e.g., after three months) to ensure the client is satisfied with the space, material, finish, hardware and to address any further questions or issues.

Key Point: The handover marks the final phase of the project, where the client receives all necessary documentation and instructions for maintaining the space. By providing clear documentation, a detailed maintenance plan, client training, and post-completion follow-ups, designers ensure the long-term success of the project.

Tool 11.7

Site Visit Checklist

A **Site Visit Checklist** is a structured list of key aspects to inspect and verify during an on-site evaluation, including measurements, material quality, work progress, and safety compliance. It ensures consistency, minimizes errors, and helps maintain project timelines.

Sn	Checklist Item	Details/Actions to Confirm	Status
1	Site Access & Security	Ensure secure access and confirm adherence to site security protocols	
2	Safety Compliance	Verify all workers are wearing necessary PPE and following safety guidelines	
3	Material Verification	Check that materials delivered match approved specifications and quality standards	
4	Workforce Skills & Competency	Ensure skilled labor is on-site and subcontractors meet required qualifications	
5	Layout & Structural Adherence	Verify the layout, framing, and structural elements align with design documents	
6	Electrical & Plumbing Rough-in	Confirm electrical and plumbing installations meet design plans and safety codes	
7	Finishes & Installations	Check installation of finishes (flooring, walls, ceilings) and fixtures as per design specs	
8	Furniture & Fixtures Placement	Ensure furniture, fixtures, and fittings are positioned and installed according to design	
9	Cabinetry & Custom Features	Inspect custom cabinetry, joinery, and other bespoke features for accuracy and quality	
10	Final Inspection & Client Approval	Conduct a final inspection, ensuring all work aligns with design intent before client approval	

Table 10.1 : Site Visit Checklist

Tool 11.8

Final Walkthrough Guide

A **Final Walkthrough Guide** is a checklist-based process that ensures all design elements, installations, and finishes meet client expectations before project completion. Mostly it's plan along with client to show the final stage of work. It helps identify any last-minute issues and ensures a smooth handover.

Room	Client Feedback	Issues to Address	Date
Living Room	Satisfied with layout and lighting, no issues.	None	N/A
Kitchen	Satisfied with layout but requests additional shelving.	Install two more shelves on the north wall.	15th June
Master Bedroom	Happy with custom wardrobe, flooring needs a touch-up.	Flooring contractor to resolve touch-up.	20th June
Guest Bedroom	Likes the design but prefers softer lighting.	Replace with warm LED lights.	18th June
Kids' Bedroom	Requests additional storage space.	Install wall-mounted cabinets above the study table.	22nd June
Dining Area	Happy with overall look but wants a larger dining table.	Order and install a bigger dining table.	25th June
Bathroom (Master)	Needs better ventilation and mirror placement adjustment.	Install an exhaust fan and reposition mirror.	17th June
Bathroom (Guest)	Faucet pressure is too low.	Plumber to inspect and fix water pressure issue.	16th June
Balcony	Wants additional greenery and better seating.	Add potted plants and install a comfortable bench.	23rd June
Foyer/ Entrance	Likes the setup but suggests better lighting.	Replace bulb with a decorative hanging light.	19th June

Table 10.2 : Final Walkthrough Guide

Conclusion

Effective **site execution** ensures that the transition from design to construction is seamless and that the project is delivered on time and to the client's satisfaction. By coordinating with contractors and suppliers, ensuring quality control, and handling on-site issues quickly, designers can mitigate challenges and maintain a high standard of work. Using tools such as the **Site Visit Checklist**, **Final Walkthrough Guide**, and **Installation Quality Control Checklist** helps streamline the process, ensuring that all tasks are tracked and quality is upheld throughout the site execution phase.

11.

Post-Project Follow-Up and Client Retention

11.1 Gathering Client Feedback and Reviews

11.2 Offering Post-Project Support and Service Plans

11.3 Securing Referrals and Repeat Business

11.4 Turning Clients Into Brand Ambassadors

11.5 Maintaining Relationships for Future Projects

Tools & Formats:

11.6 Client Satisfaction Survey

11.7 Follow-up Email Template

11.8 Referral Request Email Template

11.0

Post-Project Follow-Up and Client Retention

Executive Summary

After a project is completed, the relationship with the client doesn't end. In fact, post-project follow-up is crucial for building long-term relationships, securing future business, and strengthening your reputation in the industry. A well-handled post-project follow-up can lead to positive client reviews, referrals, repeat business, and even brand advocacy, where clients recommend your services to their network.

In this chapter, we'll explore the importance of gathering feedback, offering post-project support, obtaining referrals, and staying connected with clients for future projects. We'll also introduce essential tools such as a Client Satisfaction Survey, Post-Project Follow-Up Email Template, and Referral Request Script to help streamline these processes.

11.1

Gathering Client Feedback and Reviews

Client feedback is invaluable for improving your services and showcasing your skills to potential clients. Positive reviews and testimonials serve as social proof, enhancing your credibility and attracting new business. Gathering honest feedback also helps identify areas for improvement, ensuring that future projects run even more smoothly. By actively seeking client input, you demonstrate your commitment to quality and customer satisfaction. This fosters long-term relationships and encourages repeat business and referrals.

Best Practices for Gathering Feedback:

1. **Client Satisfaction Survey**: Use a **Client Satisfaction Survey** at the end of each project to collect feedback on various aspects of the service. Questions can cover design quality, communication, timeline adherence, and overall client satisfaction.

2. **Timing**: Send the survey within **1-2 weeks** of project completion, while the project is still fresh in the client's mind. This ensures more detailed and accurate responses.

3. **Requesting Testimonials**: For clients who are particularly happy with the outcome, politely request a **testimonial** that can be featured on your website or marketing materials. Be specific in what you're asking for, and encourage them to highlight their experience working with you.

   - In the **US** and **UK**, design firms often collect client testimonials and feature them prominently on their websites, as it has been shown to increase **conversion rates by 34%**.

   - In India, platforms like **Houzz India**, **Livspace** and **UrbanClap** are widely used for **home design reviews**. Strong reviews on these platforms can significantly boost visibility and lead generation.

Key Point: Gathering client feedback through satisfaction surveys and testimonials is crucial for improving services and building credibility. Timely requests for reviews can help boost visibility on platforms like Houzz India and Livspace. Positive testimonials, whether on your website or third-party platforms, enhance trust and attract new business.

11.2

Offering Post-Project Support and Service Plans

Providing post-project support shows your clients that you care about the long-term success of your design and not just the completion of the project. It also opens the door for **ongoing services** such as maintenance, seasonal updates, or future renovations. This commitment to continued support can lead to repeat business and valuable referrals.

Offering Post-Project Support:

1. **Service Plans**: Offer **post-project maintenance plans** that include regular check-ups or support for issues such as paint touch-ups, furniture adjustments, or appliance maintenance. These plans ensure that clients can keep their spaces in optimal condition.

   o **Example**: A **six-month post-completion visit** to assess wear and tear or suggest minor changes based on client usage patterns.

2. **Warranty Information**: Provide clients with a detailed **warranty guide** for any materials, appliances, or installations, ensuring they understand how to maintain their new space.

3. **Post-Project Check-Ins**: Set a reminder to check in with clients at **3 months and 6 months** after project completion to ensure they are happy with the space and to resolve any minor issues that may have arisen.

   o In Europe and North America, interior designers often offer a **1-year warranty period** during which clients can report any defects or issues, which are fixed at no additional charge.

   o In India, many **interior designers** and **organised interior design** firms like **Livspace, Homelane, Design Cafe** offer extended support in the form of **annual maintenance contracts (AMCs)** for high-end materials and furniture, particularly when working with imported products.

Key Point: Offering post-project support builds trust and encourages clients to reach out for additional services, fostering long-term relationships. It also helps in getting more references and positive word-of-mouth, as satisfied clients are more likely to recommend your services.

11.3

Securing Referrals and Repeat Business

Satisfied clients are one of the best sources of **referrals** and **repeat business**. A strategic approach to cultivating referrals and encouraging repeat business can significantly reduce your need for active marketing, as existing clients will become your ambassadors. Here few of the strategies one can apply:

Strategies for Securing Referrals and Repeat Business:

1. **Referral Programs**: Create a **referral program** that incentivizes clients to refer new business. For instance, you could offer a **discount** or **gift** for each successful referral that leads to a new project.

   o **Indian Reference**: In cities like Mumbai and Bangalore, many interior designers offer **referral discounts** on future projects, which are highly effective in the close-knit housing communities prevalent in urban India. For example, Livspace, an interior design platform operating in India, offers a referral program where clients earn 3% of the total project value or ₹20,000, whichever is higher, for each successful referral.

2. **Ask at the Right Time**: The best time to request referrals is after a successful project completion when the client is most satisfied. You can include a referral request in your **post-project follow-up email**.

3. **Follow-Up on Repeat Business**: When clients are happy with your work, they are more likely to return to you for **future projects**. This can be encouraged by offering services such as **seasonal updates** or **home renovations**.

   o Designers often provide **home refresh packages** every 2-3 years, allowing clients to make small updates without undergoing full-scale renovations.

Key Point: Encouraging referrals and repeat business is a cost-effective way to maintain a steady flow of clients and build long-term success. Satisfied clients are key to securing referrals and repeat business, reducing the need for active marketing. Additionally, follow-up services such as seasonal updates or home refresh packages every few years can encourage repeat clients to return for future projects.

11.4

Turning Clients into Brand Ambassadors: Building Your Reputation

When clients have an exceptional experience, they can become **brand ambassadors**, referring your services to friends, family, and colleagues. Turning clients into **advocates** for your business helps you grow organically and enhances your reputation within the industry.

Steps to Build Brand Ambassadors:

1. **Exceptional Service**: Always go **above and beyond** during the project and follow-up stages. Exceeding client expectations with attention to detail, timely communication, and thoughtful solutions creates memorable experiences that clients will want to share.

   Cutting a cake or gifting a goody bag on the handover date creates a memorable experience and helps ease any past heated discussions during the project. It's a simple yet effective way to leave a positive lasting impression.

2. **Engage on Social Media**: Ask clients to share pictures or videos of their transformed spaces on platforms like Instagram, Pinterest, and Facebook. A simple tag or hashtag can increase your brand's visibility. Interior designers like Gauri Khan Designs, Sarah Sham frequently share client projects on Instagram, often getting re-shared by happy clients, leading to more inquiries and engagement.

3. **Leverage Client Testimonials & Case Studies**: Encouraging satisfied clients to provide testimonials or participate in case studies adds credibility. Positive reviews on platforms like Google My Business, Houzz, or Justdial can influence potential customers. A 2023 survey by BrightLocal found that 87% of consumers read online reviews for local businesses before making a decision, highlighting the importance of authentic client feedback.

4. **Offer Exclusive Benefits**: Provide returning clients with **exclusive offers** or **priority service**. For example, if they refer a client, you could offer a discount on their next project or access to a special service package.

Key Point: When clients feel valued and appreciated, they are more likely to advocate for your brand and recommend you to others, further solidifying your reputation.

11.5

Maintaining Relationships for Future Projects

Maintaining a relationship with clients even after project completion can lead to future projects and referrals. **Periodic check-ins**, updates on design trends, or small service offerings can keep your brand top-of-mind and ensure long-term client loyalty.

Ways to Stay in Touch:

1. **Seasonal Greetings and Updates**: Send **seasonal greetings** (e.g., Diwali or New Year) and include a short note about any relevant design trends or updates on your business.

2. **Personalized Follow-Ups & Check-Ins**: Check in with clients a few months after project completion to ask how they're enjoying their space. This can be a simple WhatsApp message, a quick phone call, or a personalized email. Small gestures show you care beyond the project timeline. A study by Harvard Business Review found that customers who feel a personal connection with a brand are 52% more valuable in terms of repeat business and referrals.

3. **Offer Design Updates**: Periodically suggest **small updates** that could refresh their space, such as new color palettes, furniture upgrades, or re-arrangements. This can create opportunities for new projects.

4. **Exclusive Client Events & Workshops:** Hosting exclusive events—such as a home décor workshop or a sneak peek into upcoming design trends—keeps clients engaged. Design firms like Asian Paints' Beautiful Homes frequently organize décor workshops, keeping clients connected while subtly promoting new offerings.

5. **Email Newsletters**: Send **quarterly newsletters** to keep clients informed about your latest projects, design tips like "How to prepare your home for summer" , "10 must have wardrobe organisers" or "2025 Interior Design Trends."

Key Point: Consistent communication keeps your brand relevant to clients, increasing the likelihood of future collaborations and referrals .Building a long-term relationship with clients through personalized follow-ups, exclusive experiences, and valuable insights strengthens client loyalty and creates more business opportunities.

Tool 11.6

Client Satisfaction Survey Form

A **Client Satisfaction Survey Form** is a tool used to gather feedback from clients about their experience with a service or product. It helps businesses assess performance, identify areas for improvement, and enhance customer relationships.

CLIENT SATISFACTION SURVEY FORM		
Dear Sir/Madam. Thank you for choosing our services! Your feedback is invaluable in helping us improve. Please take a few minutes to rate your experience.		
Category	**Rating (1-5)**	**Comments**
Design Quality & Aesthetics	☐ 1 ☐ 2 ☐ 3 ☐ 4 ☐ 5	
Functionality & Practicality	☐ 1 ☐ 2 ☐ 3 ☐ 4 ☐ 5	
Understanding of Your Requirements	☐ 1 ☐ 2 ☐ 3 ☐ 4 ☐ 5	
Communication & Responsiveness	☐ 1 ☐ 2 ☐ 3 ☐ 4 ☐ 5	
Timeliness of Project Completion	☐ 1 ☐ 2 ☐ 3 ☐ 4 ☐ 5	
Budget Adherence	☐ 1 ☐ 2 ☐ 3 ☐ 4 ☐ 5	
Problem-Solving & Adaptability	☐ 1 ☐ 2 ☐ 3 ☐ 4 ☐ 5	
Workmanship & Material Quality	☐ 1 ☐ 2 ☐ 3 ☐ 4 ☐ 5	
Post-Completion Support & Service	☐ 1 ☐ 2 ☐ 3 ☐ 4 ☐ 5	
Overall Experience	☐ 1 ☐ 2 ☐ 3 ☐ 4 ☐ 5	
Design Quality & Aesthetics	☐ 1 ☐ 2 ☐ 3 ☐ 4 ☐ 5	
Functionality & Practicality	☐ 1 ☐ 2 ☐ 3 ☐ 4 ☐ 5	
Rating Scale: 1 - Poor | 2 - Fair | 3 - Good | 4 - Very Good | 5 - Excellent		
Would you recommend our services to others? ☐ Yes ☐ No		
What areas do you think we could improve on? ______________________		

Table 11.1 : Client Satisfaction Survey Form

Tool 11.7

Post-Project Follow-Up Email Template

A Post-Project Follow-Up Email should be sent within a few days to a week after project completion to express gratitude, gather client feedback, and offer post-project support. This helps maintain a positive relationship, improve future services, and encourage referrals.

Sample Email Template

Subject: Thank You and Follow-Up on Your [Project Name]

Dear [Client Name],

I hope you're enjoying your newly designed space! It was a pleasure working with you, and I'm truly grateful for the opportunity to bring your vision to life.

As part of our commitment to continuous improvement, we'd love to hear your thoughts. Please take a few minutes to complete our Client Satisfaction Survey, which helps us enhance our services and better meet client needs.

The survey is simple and takes only 5 minutes to complete. You'll be asked to rate different aspects of the project—such as design quality, communication, timeliness, and overall satisfaction—on a scale of 1 to 5, where:

1 - Poor | 2 - Fair | 3 - Good | 4 - Very Good | 5 - Excellent

Additionally, there's space for you to share any comments or suggestions. Your feedback is invaluable in helping us refine our services. Click here to complete the survey: [Insert Survey Link]

If you have any further questions or need post-project assistance, please feel free to reach out. Also, if you know anyone who might be interested in our services, we would be incredibly grateful for your referrals!

Thank you once again for choosing [Your Company Name]. I look forward to staying in touch and hopefully working together again in the future.

Best   **regards,**
[Your Name] & [Your Contact]

Tool 11.8

Referral Request Email

A Referral Request Email is a professional yet friendly message sent to past clients, asking them to recommend your services to friends, family, or colleagues. It serves as a strategic way to generate new business through word-of-mouth marketing. This email: Encourages satisfied clients to share their positive experience with others Offers an incentive (such as discounts or free consultations) to motivate referrals. Strengthens client relationships by keeping communication open even after project completion. Helps grow your business organically with trusted recommendations.!

Sample Email Template

Subject: Share the Joy – Referral Appreciation!

Dear [Client Name],

I hope you're loving your newly designed space! It was a pleasure working with you, and I truly appreciate the trust you placed in me to bring your vision to life.

I wanted to reach out because many of my clients come through personal referrals, and I'd love the opportunity to help your friends, family, or colleagues create their dream spaces as well. If you know someone who might be interested in interior design services, I would be grateful for your recommendation.

As a token of appreciation, for every referral that leads to a new project, I'd love to offer you [a discount on your next service OR a complimentary design consultation]. It's my way of saying thank you for your support and trust.

If someone comes to mind, feel free to share my contact details or simply reply to this email with their name, and I'd be happy to reach out personally.

Thank you again for choosing [Your Company Name]. Your recommendation means the world to me, and I look forward to the possibility of working together again in the future!

Best **regards,**
[Your Name] & [Your Contact]

Conclusion

Building lasting relationships after the project concludes is vital for ensuring **client satisfaction**, securing **referrals**, and encouraging **repeat business**. By gathering feedback, offering post-project support, and staying in touch, designers can turn clients into long-term partners and advocates. Using tools such as the **Client Satisfaction Survey**, **Post-Project Follow-Up Email Template**, and **Referral Request Email** designers can maintain clear communication with clients, ensuring strong relationships that benefit both parties for years to come.

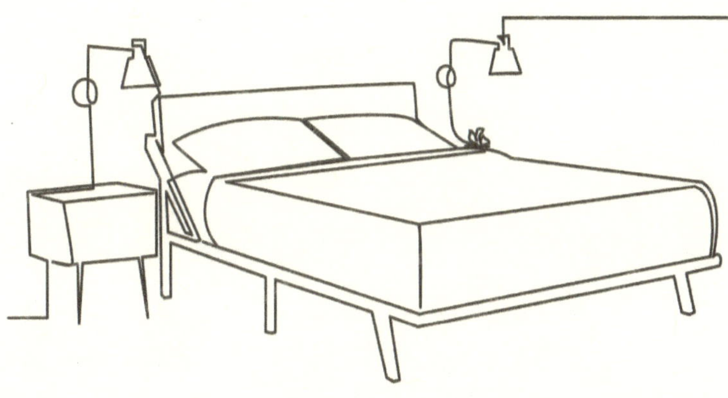

12.

Financial Essentials for Interior Designers

12.1 Importance of Financial Knowledge for Designers

12.2 How to Calculate Profit and Margin?

12.3 Why to Charge Design Fees?

12.4 Why to Take an Advance in Design Fees ?

12.5 Handling Price Increases or Fluctuations

Scan here
for more
digital
content

12.0

Financial Essentials for Interior Designers

Executive Summary

Financial knowledge is essential for interior designers, especially those involved in sales and business operations. Understanding key financial concepts helps designers set competitive pricing, manage project costs, and ensure profitability while maintaining client trust. This chapter covers the fundamental financial principles every interior designer should know, from calculating profit margins to handling price fluctuations. By mastering these concepts, designers can make informed business decisions, communicate value effectively to clients, and secure sustainable revenue.

The chapter explores crucial aspects such as why charging design fees is necessary, the importance of taking advance payments, and how to navigate unexpected price fluctuations in materials and labor costs. Designers will learn practical strategies to maintain cash flow, negotiate with suppliers, and protect project profitability. Equipped with these financial insights, designers can build a strong foundation for long-term success while enhancing client satisfaction and trust.

12.1

Importance of Financial Knowledge for Interior Designers

For interior designers involved in sales, financial literacy is essential for setting the right prices, managing project budgets, and ensuring profitability. Understanding financial concepts helps designers communicate value to clients, handle negotiations confidently, and make informed business decisions. Without financial knowledge, designers may struggle with pricing errors, cash flow issues, or tax complications, ultimately affecting the firm's success

Key Financial Concepts an Interior Designer in Sales Should Know

- **Pricing Strategies:** Understanding how to price services accurately ensures profitability. Designers must factor in material costs, labor, overhead, and desired profit margins to set competitive yet sustainable prices.

- **Profit Margins and Markups:** Profit margins indicate how much a designer earns after covering all costs. Markups on materials and furnishings contribute to additional revenue.

- **Budgeting and Cost Control:** A designer must track material, labor, and operational costs to avoid budget overruns. Effective cost control helps maintain profitability and avoid financial losses.

- **GST and Tax Compliance:** Interior design services in India attract 18% GST. Designers must charge GST on invoices, claim Input Tax Credit (ITC), and file GST returns.

- **Managing Cash Flow:** Cash flow management ensures that a designer has enough funds to pay for materials, labor, and expenses before receiving full client payments.

- **Negotiation Skills Based on Financial Understanding:** A designer must negotiate prices with vendors and clients to maximize profitability. Understanding costs helps in confidently justifying prices and offering discounts without affecting margins.

- **Financial Record-Keeping and Software Tools:** Accurate financial records help in tax filing, profitability analysis, and expense tracking. For example,

  - Tally ERP / QuickBooks: For invoicing and bookkeeping.

- Google Sheets / Excel: For tracking budgets and profit margins.

- Houzz Pro: For managing design project finances.

- **Understanding Return on Investment (ROI):** Every design choice should be evaluated based on client expectations and financial returns. ROI measures the effectiveness of design investments, helping designers pitch high-value solutions to clients.

- **Avoiding Common Financial Mistake:**

  - Underpricing Services: Leads to unsustainable business operations.

  - Ignoring GST Compliance: Results in legal penalties.

  - Poor Cash` Flow Management: Causes delays in vendor payments.

  - No Profit Tracking: Leads to unexpected financial losses.

- **Business Growth and Scaling:** With proper financial knowledge, designers can plan for business expansion by analyzing revenue streams, reinvesting profits, and scaling services efficiently.

12.2

How to Calculate Profit and Margin?

Understanding Key Financial Terms:

Before diving into calculations, let's define some essential terms:

1. **Total Project Cost (TPC)** – The total amount you charge the client for the project, including materials, labor, and your fees.
2. **Material Cost (MC)** – The cost incurred for purchasing raw materials, furniture, fixtures, and accessories.
3. **Labor Cost (LC)** – The cost of hiring contractors, carpenters, painters, and other workers.
4. **Overhead Costs (OC)** – Indirect costs such as office rent, salaries of staff, electricity, software subscriptions, and marketing.
5. **Profit (P)** – The amount remaining after deducting all costs from the total project cost.
6. **Margin (%)** – The percentage of the selling price that is profit.

How to calculate Profit?:

Profit = Total Project Cost − (Material Cost + Labor Cost + Overhead Costs + Taxes)

How to calculate Margin (%)?:

Margin = (Profit / Total Project Cost) x 100

Step-by-Step Profit & Margin Calculation with Example

Let study an example, an interior designer is working on a 2BHK home interior project with a Total Project Cost (TPC) of ₹10,00,000. The budget is allocated across different cost components:

Material Cost (MC) of ₹4,00,000, covering furniture, lighting, and decor; Labor Cost (LC) of ₹2,00,000, including carpenters, electricians, and painters; and Overhead Costs (OC) of ₹1,00,000, accounting for design software, transportation, and office expenses. Additionally, GST at 18% is applied on the total selling price, impacting the final billing amount.

Step 1: Calculate Pre-GST Project Revenue, Since GST (18%) is included in the total project cost, we must first extract the base amount.
Base Amount = (TPC / 1.18) = (10,000,00 / 1.18) = Rs 8,47,457 /-
Step 2: Calculate Total Costs by summing up all Direct and Indirect costs like material, labor and overhead costs.
Total Cost = (MC+LC+OC) = (4,000,00+2,00,00+1,00,00) = Rs 7,00,000 /-
Step 3: Now Calculate Profit
Profit = (Base Amount - Total Cost) = (8,47,457 - 7,70,000) = Rs 1,47,457 /-
Step 4: Now Calculate Margin
Margin = (Profit / Base Amount) x 100 = (147,457 / 8,47,457) x 100 = 17.4%

12.3

Why to Charge Design Fees?

Charging design fees is crucial for interior designers as it reflects their expertise, time, and creative effort. A well-structured fee ensures that the designer is fairly compensated for their work, covering consultation, concept development, planning, and project coordination. Without charging a design fee, a designer risks undervaluing their services and relying solely on product markups, which can be inconsistent and unsustainable.

Key Reasons an Interior Designer Should Charge Design Fees:

- **Professional Compensation for Expertise:** Designers bring creativity, industry knowledge, and technical skills to transform a space. Charging a design fee ensures they are paid for their expertise rather than relying only on material sales. For example a designer spends 40+ hours planning a 2BHK apartment, creating mood boards, selecting materials, and drafting layouts. A design fee ensures fair compensation for this time.

- **Time Investment in Client Projects:** Interior design involves consultations, site visits, vendor coordination, and multiple revisions. A design fee covers the extensive time spent on each project. For example a designer working on a ₹15,00,000 project spends weeks finalizing concepts. If they don't charge a design fee, they may not be adequately paid for this effort.

- **Ensuring Commitment from Clients:** A design fee filters out non-serious inquiries, ensuring that only committed clients proceed with the project. This prevents wasted time on indecisive clients. For example charging an initial consultation fee of ₹5,000 - ₹10,000 ensures that the client values the designer's time and expertise.

- **Covering Business and Operational Costs:** Running an interior design business involves expenses like software, office rent, staff salaries, and marketing. A design fee contributes to covering these operational costs.

- **Reducing Dependence on Product Sales:** Many designers earn through commissions on furniture, lighting, and décor sales, but this can be unpredictable. A design fee ensures steady income regardless of product sales.

12.4

Why to Take an Advance in Design Fees?

Taking an advance payment before beginning design services is a professional practice that benefits both the designer and the client. It secures the designer's time, ensures financial stability, and signifies a serious commitment from the client. Without an advance, designers risk investing time and effort without guaranteed compensation.

Key Reasons an Interior Designer Should Take an Advance Fee:

- **Ensures Serious Commitment from Clients:** An advance payment filters out non-serious inquiries and ensures the client is genuinely interested in proceeding with the project.

- **Covers Initial Design and Consultation Costs:** Interior design involves research, site visits, and conceptualization, which require time and resources. An advance payment ensures these efforts are compensated.

- **Secures Cash Flow for Business Operations:** Design firms incur expenses such as software licenses, staff salaries, and overhead costs. An advance payment provides working capital to cover these essential expenses.

- **Prevents Project Abandonment:** Without an advance, a client may delay or abandon the project after initial discussions, leaving the designer with unpaid work.

- **Strengthens Professionalism and Industry Standards:** Reputable designers and firms worldwide follow the practice of collecting advance payments. It sets clear financial expectations and fosters trust between the client and designer.

How to Ask for an Advance Payment Professionally?

Clients may hesitate if they don't understand why an advance is required. A clear, professional explanation helps build trust.

- **Explain the Industry Standard:** As per industry practices, we require a [percentage]% advance to secure the project. This ensures a smooth workflow and allows us to dedicate resources exclusively to your design.

- **Highlight the Work Involved:** Designing involves research, site visits, and expert planning before execution begins. An advance covers these initial efforts to ensure a high-quality outcome.

- **Provide a Breakdown of Costs:** The advance helps us allocate resources for concept development, 3D designs, and project planning. It also covers initial expenses such as material samples and vendor coordination.

- **Offer Payment Flexibility:** We provide payment milestones so you can make payments progressively as the project advances.

Key Point: Taking an advance payment before starting a project ensures financial stability, serious client commitment, and fair compensation for the designer's time and expertise. Using industry-standard methods such as percentage-based advances, fixed booking fees, or milestone payments, designers can maintain professionalism while making clients comfortable with the payment process.

12.5

Handling Price Increases or Fluctuations?

Price fluctuations are a common challenge in interior design projects due to factors such as market demand, material shortages, labor cost variations, and government-imposed taxes. A designer must be prepared to manage these fluctuations effectively to ensure profitability while maintaining client trust.

Key Strategies for Handling Sourcing Side Price Increases:

- **Lock Prices Early with Vendors and Suppliers:** Negotiating fixed-price contracts with vendors helps secure pricing for materials and furnishings in advance, reducing the impact of sudden price hikes.

- **Use Multiple Suppliers to Compare and Optimize Costs:** Sourcing materials from different vendors allows designers to switch suppliers if one increases prices unexpectedly.

- **Pre-Purchase High-Risk Items:** Certain materials, like imported lighting fixtures or wooden flooring, are prone to price volatility. Pre-purchasing such items at an agreed rate can protect the project budget.

- **Establish Long-Term Relationships with Suppliers:** Building strong relationships with key vendors can help designers secure better credit terms, early discounts, and priority pricing during fluctuations.

- **Use Alternative Materials When Prices Spike:** If a specific material becomes too expensive, designers can offer alternatives that maintain the design aesthetic while staying within budget.

Key Strategies for Managing Price Increases with Client:

- **Set Price Validity Periods in Quotations:** Including a price validity clause (e.g., valid for 15-30 days) in proposals prevents clients from delaying decisions while expecting the same pricing months later.

- **Educate Clients About Market Fluctuations:** Explaining to clients that material and labor costs fluctuate due to factors like inflation and demand helps set realistic expectations.

- **Offer Multiple Budget Options**: Providing clients with different budget scenarios allows flexibility in managing unexpected price hikes.

- **Adjust the Payment Schedule to Accommodate Increases:** Breaking the project into phases allows designers to adjust prices incrementally instead of increasing the full project cost upfront.

- **Offer Clients Fixed-Price Packages for Predictability:** Some clients prefer fixed-cost packages to avoid unexpected increases. Designers can include a margin to absorb minor fluctuations while keeping the price stable for the client.

How to Communicate Price Increases to Clients Professionally?

Clients may resist price increases, so it's essential to explain them transparently. A clear document with terms and conditions with client is the key for such situation.

- **Provide Clear Data and Justification:** Due to a 12% increase in labor costs and a 15% rise in tile prices, the total project cost has been adjusted accordingly. We are happy to explore cost-saving alternatives if needed.

- Offer Solutions Instead of Just Stating the Increase: To stay within budget despite the increase in wood prices, we can explore high-quality engineered wood as an alternative.

- Maintain a Positive and Professional Approach: We understand that cost increases can be challenging, and we are committed to finding the best value without compromising on quality."

Key Point: Handling price fluctuations effectively requires proactive planning, vendor negotiations, educating clients, and offering flexible solutions. By locking prices early, using multiple suppliers, setting price validity periods, and offering alternatives, designers can navigate cost increases while maintaining a positive client relationship and ensuring project profitability.

Conclusion:

Financial literacy is not just an added skill but a necessity for interior designers looking to run a profitable business. By understanding pricing structures, profit margins, and cost management strategies, designers can confidently navigate project budgets and client negotiations. Charging appropriate design fees and securing advance payments ensures financial stability, while strategic planning helps mitigate risks from market fluctuations. Ultimately, a solid grasp of financial essentials empowers designers to make informed decisions, sustain profitability, and build lasting client relationships in the competitive interior design industry.

13.

Competitive Positioning and Sales Negotiation

13.1 How to Compare and Explain Quotes to Clients?

13.2 Negotiation Tactics: Handling Discount Requests

13.3 Handling Last-Minute Changes to Design or Budget

Scan here
for more
digital
content

13.0

Competitive Positioning and Sales Negotiation

Executive Summary

In the competitive world of interior design, effectively positioning your services and mastering sales negotiation are essential skills for winning projects and maintaining profitability. Clients often compare multiple quotes, request discounts, and make last-minute changes, making it crucial for designers to confidently present their value. This chapter provides insights on how to compare and explain quotes transparently, helping clients understand key differences such as branded vs. non-branded materials, GST compliance, warranty terms, and design specifications. By educating clients on these factors, designers can build trust and justify their pricing, ensuring fair compensation for their expertise.

Additionally, sales negotiations play a vital role in closing deals while protecting profit margins. This chapter explores practical tactics for handling discount requests without devaluing services, offering strategic alternatives like phased execution, value-added benefits, and transparent cost breakdowns. Lastly, managing last-minute changes efficiently—whether in design or budget—ensures smooth project execution. By setting clear expectations, documenting modifications, and providing cost-effective alternatives, designers can maintain control while keeping clients satisfied.

13.1

How to Compare and Explain Quotes to Clients

When clients receive multiple quotes for their interior design project, they often focus on the total cost rather than understanding the value, quality, and scope of services included. As an interior designer, it is crucial to help clients compare quotes effectively and explain why your pricing is justified. This approach builds trust and prevents misunderstandings that could arise from a price-only comparison.

Key Factors in Comparing Quotes:

A lower-priced quote may appear attractive but could lead to hidden costs, poor material quality, or lack of after-sales support. Here's how to guide your clients in evaluating quotes beyond just the final amount:

- **Scope of Work and Service Inclusions:** Some quotes may include comprehensive services like design consultation, 3D visualizations, project supervision, and post-installation support, while others might only cover the basic design.

- **Example:**
  - **Designer A (₹3,00,000):** Includes detailed drawings, multiple revisions, 3D renders, site visits, and vendor coordination.
  - **Designer B (₹2,50,000):** Offers only basic 2D plans and leaves material procurement and labor supervision to the client.
  - **Tip:** A detailed and transparent scope prevents clients from choosing an incomplete service package just because it seems cheaper.

- **Material Specifications:** (Branded vs. Non-Branded): Material quality plays a critical role in both aesthetics and durability. Quotes may differ based on whether branded or generic materials are used.

- **Example:**
  - **Plywood:** Branded marine-grade plywood (century/greenply) vs. local commercial plywood with no moisture resistance.
  - **Hardware:** Hettich/Hafele/Blum soft-close hinges and channels vs. local hardware that wears out quickly.
  - **Kitchen Countertops:** Quartz/Granite vs. local marble
  - **Tip:** Explain that branded materials come with manufacturer warranties and long-term durability, reducing future repair costs.

- **Number of Drawers vs. Doors in Kitchen Units:** Cabinet construction and hardware choices significantly impact the cost and usability of a kitchen.

- **Example:**

  - **Kitchen with more drawers:** Offers better ergonomics and storage efficiency, but costs more due to extra hardware (soft-close channels).
  - **Kitchen with more doors:** Cheaper but may require bending frequently to access stored items.
  - **Tip:** Show clients how practicality and convenience justify a slightly higher cost.

- **Type of Surface Finish:** (Laminate vs. Acrylic vs. PU Paint): Different finishes impact cost, maintenance, and longevity.

- **Example:**

  - **Glossy Laminate:** Affordable, easy maintenance, but limited premium feel.

  - **Acrylic Finish:** Expensive, luxurious, scratch-resistant, and durable.
  - **PU Paint Finish:** Highest cost, seamless finish, customizable but requires careful maintenance.
  - **Tip:** Let clients feel samples to understand the difference in touch and durability.

- **Core Material Thickness and Quality:** The thickness of core panels used in furniture impacts durability, stability, and cost.

- **Example:**

  - 18mm thick plywood (standard) vs. 16mm or 12mm plywood (cheaper but less durable).

  - MDF for wardrobes (cost-effective) vs. HDF (more durable, moisture-resistant).

  - **Tip:** Highlight how thicker, better-quality panels prevent bending and sagging over time.

- **Warranty and Hidden Clauses:** Lower-cost quotes may not include a proper warranty for materials or workmanship, leading to unexpected repair costs.

- **Example:**
    - **Quote A:** 5-year warranty on modular kitchen hardware, service charges, replacement terms, furniture, clear policy on what is covered.
    - **Quote B:** "Warranty included" but only covers factory defects, not daily wear and tear.
    - **Tip:** Always ask for written warranties, misleading informations and explain hidden clauses that may make a low-cost quote misleading.

- **Taxes: No GST vs. GST-Inclusive Pricing:** Some vendors avoid GST to make their quotes appear cheaper, mostly unorganised interior designer or freelance designers without having a registered firm do not have any GST numbers, but this can lead to issues with billing transparency and legal compliance.

- **Example:**
    - **Quote A** (With GST): Proper tax invoice, eligible for business deductions, compliant with government regulations.
    - **Quote B** (Without GST): No tax invoice, potential legal risks, no accountability if issues arise.
    - **Tip:** Clients may save on tax claims when they opt for a proper invoice with GST.

- **Project Timeline and Site Supervision:** Faster project execution often involves better planning and dedicated supervision, while delays can increase indirect costs for the client. Unorganised designers or interior decorators never put a deadline to their projects. The long duration of project at site not only incur more indirect cost but also add lots of discomfort to the client. An organised player always complete the site on given timeline and if not then surely put a penalty clause to protect the customer deadlines.

- **Example:**
    - **Designer A:** (₹1,00,000 higher): Project completed in 60 days with a dedicated project manager.
    - **Designer B**: Lower cost, but delays up to 90 days due to lack of site coordination.
    - **Tip:** Explain how faster completion reduces rental costs, inconvenience, and stress.

How to Present the Comparison to Client?

Once you've identified the differences, structure your explanation clearly:

Step 1: Present a Comparison Table: Use a side-by-side breakdown to highlight the value of your quote.

Component	Your Quote (₹)	Competitor Quote (₹)	Notes
Design Consultation	50,000	40,000	Includes 3D renders, unlimited revisions
Kitchen Plywood (18mm)	1,50,000	1,20,000	Branded vs. local plywood
Hardware (Soft-Close)	45,000	30,000	Hettich vs. generic brand
Wardrobe Finish (Acrylic)	70,000	55,000	Premium acrylic vs. laminate
Site Supervision	Included	Not Included	Ensures quality control
Warranty	5 Years	1 Year	Clear vs. hidden clauses
GST	Included	Not Included	Legal invoice, tax benefits

Table 13.1 : Quote Comparison Table

Step 2: Educate Clients on Value, Not Just Cost: Instead of justifying your pricing, explain how it benefits them in the long run.

"While our quote is slightly higher, it includes high-quality materials, better hardware, and a 5-year warranty, ensuring durability and long-term savings."

Step 3: Offer Flexible Budget Adjustments: If a client has budget concerns, suggest cost-saving alternatives without compromising quality.

"We can switch to a high-quality laminate instead of acrylic, which reduces costs without affecting durability."

Step 4: Reinforce Credibility with Testimonials: Share real-life examples of clients who initially chose cheaper options but later regretted it.

"One of our clients opted for a lower quote but later faced issues with peeling laminates and weak hinges. They eventually had to redo the work at a higher cost."

Key Point: Comparing and explaining quotes is about educating clients on value, transparency, and long-term benefits. By breaking down costs effectively, highlighting quality differences, and addressing common concerns, designers can justify their pricing and help clients make informed decisions.

13.2

Negotiation Tactics: Handling Discount Requests

Negotiation is an inevitable part of sales in interior design. Clients often request discounts, either to fit their budget, compare with competitors, or simply as a bargaining habit. As a designer responsible for closing sales, it's important to handle discount requests professionally while protecting your profit margins and maintaining the perceived value of your services. The key is to justify your pricing, offer smart alternatives, and create a win-win situation without undercutting your business.

Understanding Why Clients Ask for Discounts: Clients may request discounts for various reasons:

- **Budget Constraints:** They genuinely want your services but have a fixed budget. This can be a real issue with service class customer, hence need to handle carefully.

- **Comparison with Other Quotes:** They have received a lower price from another designer or vendor. Client can not compare technical quotes so its a good opportunity to compare and explain the major differences between your and competitor quote.

- **Cultural Habit:** Some clients negotiate by default, assuming prices are flexible. This comes from a general client behaviour as everyone likes to negotiate.

- **Perceived High Pricing:** They don't fully understand the quality or value included in your proposal. In such case you need to explain using value and benefit formulas.

Instead of immediately lowering your price, first understand their concerns and address them strategically. Here are give few examples which will help in understanding how to revert or behave in such situations without loosing deal.

Negotiation Strategies for Handling Discount Requests

- **Justify the Value Instead of Reducing Price:** Many clients ask for discounts because they don't fully understand what they are paying for. Before considering any price reduction, ensure they see the value of your services and materials.

- **Example:**
  - "Our quote includes high-quality materials like branded plywood, soft-close hardware, and a 5-year service warranty. Choosing a lower quote might mean compromising on these, which could lead to higher maintenance costs later."
  - **Tip:** Use comparison tables, testimonials, and real-life examples to reinforce the benefits of your pricing.

- **Offer Cost-Saving Alternatives Instead of Discounts:** If the client insists on a lower price, suggest budget-friendly alternatives instead of reducing your profit

- **Example:**
  - Instead of acrylic finishes, offer high-quality laminates to reduce costs.
  - Instead of imported marble, suggest engineered quartz that looks premium but is more affordable.
  - Reduce excessive custom elements like detailed carvings and CNC work.
  - **Tip:** This approach satisfies the client's budget needs while keeping your profit intact

- **Create Value-Added Offers Instead of Discount:** Rather than cutting prices, add small complementary services that make the client feel they are getting a better deal.

- **Example:**
  - Free Consultation for a Future Space: "If you go ahead with this project, I'll include a free consultation for your next room renovation."
  - Extended Warranty: "I can extend the warranty from 3 years to 5 years at no extra cost."
  - Complimentary Décor Styling: "We can offer a one-time soft-furnishing styling service after project completion."
  - **Tip:** It makes the client feel getting more value without reducing your pricing.

- **Use Payment Flexibility as a Negotiation Tool:** Sometimes, clients request discounts because they are facing cash flow constraints. Instead of lowering your fees, offer flexible payment terms.

- **Example:**
    - Instead of a ₹5,00,000 one-time payment, offer three installments of ₹1,66,000 each.
    - Offer a small discount for upfront full payment, ensuring your cash flow remains stable.
    - **Tip:** This allows the client to manage their budget without affecting your profitability

- **Politely Hold Your Ground When Necessary:** Some clients may push aggressively for discounts. In such cases, remain firm while being professional.

- **Example:**
    - "I understand your concern, and I would love to work on this project. However, we have carefully priced our services to ensure high-quality materials and execution. Reducing the price further would compromise the quality, which we don't recommend."
    - **Tip:** Clients respect designers who stand by their pricing confidently rather than agreeing to discounts too easily.

- **Use Scarcity and Urgency to Close the Deal:** A subtle way to avoid endless negotiations is by introducing a time-sensitive offer to encourage a quick decision.

- **Example:**
    - "We have a price revision coming up next month, so confirming now ensures you lock in the current rate."
    - "I have only one slot available for this project timeline, and I'd love to book it for you before it gets filled."
    - **Tip:** Scarcity makes clients act faster and commit without excessive bargaining.

Apart from above the designer must address competitor price comparisons smartly, if a client says, "I got a lower quote elsewhere," don't rush to match it. Instead, analyze the competitor's offer and highlight missing elements. It is often observed that clients are more likely to act in your favor when you provide them with clear and transparent information, rather than simply offering discounts to close the deal.

How to Respond to Common Discount Requests?

Here is a table with some common client requests during discount negotiations, along with smart responses to handle them effectively.

Client's Request	How to Respond
"Can you lower your price?"	"Our pricing is based on high-quality materials, expert craftsmanship, and project management to ensure the best results. Would you like to explore some material options to adjust the budget?"
"Your competitor is charging less."	"Let's compare what's included in both quotes. Often, a lower price means lower-quality materials or hidden costs."
"Can I get a 10% discount?"	"Instead of a direct discount, I can offer you an additional post-completion check-in service at no extra cost."
"I have a limited budget."	"I understand. Let's prioritize the essential elements and see where we can optimize costs without compromising quality."
"I will refer more clients if you give me a discount."	"We truly appreciate referrals! Once we successfully complete your project, we'd be happy to discuss a referral benefit for future projects."
"Can you match the price offered by another designer?"	"I appreciate you considering multiple options. Our pricing reflects the quality of materials, design expertise, and personalized service we provide. I'd be happy to walk you through the differences so you can make an informed decision."

Table 13.2 : Ways to Respond to Common Discount Requests

Key Point: Negotiation is not about lowering prices but about reinforcing the value of your services, offering smart alternatives, and ensuring a fair deal for both parties. By handling discount requests confidently and professionally, interior designers can close sales profitably while maintaining client trust and satisfaction.

13.3

Handling Last-Minute Changes to Design or Budget

Interior design projects are dynamic, and last-minute changes from clients are common. Whether it's a sudden budget cut or a design modification, handling these requests efficiently while maintaining project quality and profitability is crucial. Designers must be prepared with strategies to accommodate reasonable changes while protecting their timelines and financial interests.

1. Understanding the Reason for the Change: Before making adjustments, it's essential to understand why the client is requesting a change. Common reasons include:

- Budget constraints due to unexpected expenses elsewhere.
- New inspirations or preferences discovered mid-project.
- Unavailability of specific materials or finishes.
- Influence from family members or consultants.
- **Tip:** A quick discussion to understand the priority behind the change can help determine the best course of action.

2. Managing Budget Reductions Without Compromising Quality: If the client wants to reduce costs at the last minute, consider these strategies:

- Adjust material selection: Switching from high-end finishes like acrylic to premium laminates can reduce costs without sacrificing aesthetics.
- Optimize design elements: Reducing the number of drawers in kitchen cabinets and replacing them with doors can cut hardware costs significantly.
- Reevaluate scope: Offer phased execution where non-essential items can be implemented later.
- Suggest alternative vendors: Exploring alternative suppliers or brands for fixtures and furnishings can sometimes provide cost savings.

3. Handling Changes in Design Elements: Clients may request modifications that impact layouts, materials, or aesthetics. Address these effectively by:

- Clarifying feasibility: Some changes may require structural modifications or additional approvals. Explaining the impact of these changes on other areas of the home helps clients understand the broader implications and make informed decisions.

- Highlighting impact on cost & schedule: Explain how changes may affect the project budget and timeline. For example, switching to a custom-built wardrobe instead of a modular one might extend the delivery timeline by weeks.
- Using Change Orders: Document design modifications with a formal change order, including revised costs and approval from the client.

4. Addressing Material & Vendor Availability Issues: Sometimes, material shortages or vendor delays can force last-minute changes. To mitigate this:

- Have backup options: Always shortlist alternative materials with similar aesthetics and durability.
- Communicate early: If a particular brand of hardware is unavailable, notify the client with comparable alternatives before delays occur.
- Regularly check stock at vendors: For frequently used materials and hardware, maintain regular stock checks with vendors to ensure availability and avoid unexpected shortages.
- Negotiate with suppliers: In cases where vendor prices increase unexpectedly, negotiate bulk discounts or explore different vendor or sources.

5. Handling Unrealistic Client Demand: Not all last-minute changes are practical or cost-effective. If a client requests unrealistic modifications:

- Set clear boundaries: Politely but firmly explain what is possible within the existing scope.
- Offer expert advice: Educate the client on why certain changes may not be beneficial in the long run.
- Provide alternatives: If the desired change is unfeasible, suggest solutions that align with the budget and timeline.

6. Communicating Proactively to Avoid Last-Minute Changes: Preventing last-minute changes is always better than reacting to them. Strategies to minimize unexpected revisions include:

- Frequent design approvals: Break down the project into stages where clients sign off on designs before execution.
- Material mockups & samples: Letting clients physically see and feel materials before installation can reduce later dissatisfaction.
- Transparent budgeting: Providing a clear cost breakdown early on helps clients make informed decisions.

Key Point: Handling last-minute changes requires a balance between flexibility and control. By assessing the feasibility, communicating cost and timeline implications, and using structured approval processes, designers can manage modifications without compromising project success.

Conclusion

Competitive positioning and sales negotiation are critical components of a successful interior design business. By clearly explaining price differences, confidently handling discount requests, and strategically managing last-minute changes, designers can establish themselves as professionals who deliver both quality and value. The ability to educate clients, set boundaries, and communicate proactively not only strengthens client relationships but also ensures long-term profitability. Mastering these techniques helps designers navigate challenges smoothly, close deals effectively, and maintain a strong market position in the ever-evolving interior design industry.

14.

Ethics and Professional Standards in Interior Design

14.1 Code of Ethics for Interior Designers

14.2 Maintaining Transparency with Clients

14.3 Confidentiality and Intellectual Property

14.0

Ethics and Professional Standards in Interior Design

Executive Summary

Ethics and professionalism are the foundation of a reputable and sustainable interior design practice. Clients trust designers with their spaces, investments, and personal preferences, making it crucial to uphold integrity, fairness, and transparency in all interactions. This chapter explores the essential ethical standards interior designers must follow, from adhering to industry codes of conduct to ensuring honesty in pricing, material selection, and project execution. Upholding these principles not only enhances credibility but also builds long-term client relationships and strengthens the profession as a whole.

Maintaining transparency with clients is another key aspect of ethical design practice. Providing clear contracts, explaining pricing breakdowns, and setting realistic expectations prevent misunderstandings and foster trust. Additionally, protecting client confidentiality and intellectual property is vital, as designers often work with sensitive information and proprietary concepts. This chapter outlines best practices for safeguarding project details, ensuring fair usage rights, and maintaining professional integrity. By committing to high ethical standards, designers can elevate their reputation, avoid disputes, and create a positive industry impact.

14.1

Code of Ethics for Interior Designers

A strong ethical foundation is essential for every interior designer to build credibility and trust with clients, suppliers, and peers. Professionalism in design goes beyond aesthetics—it requires honesty, integrity, and a commitment to fair practices. Various industry organizations, such as the Council for Interior Design Qualification (CIDQ) and The Indian Institute of Interior Designers (IIID), have established ethical guidelines that every designer should follow.

Key Ethical Principles for Interior Designers:

- **Honesty and Fairness:** Always provide truthful information about services, pricing, and material quality. Misrepresentation of costs or capabilities can damage credibility.

- **Client-Centered Approach:** Prioritize client needs while maintaining professional boundaries. Avoid conflicts of interest or biased recommendations for personal gain.

- **Transparency in Pricing:** Clearly outline all costs, including materials, labor, and additional charges. Hidden fees erode trust and lead to disputes.

- **Respect for Contracts and Agreements:** Honor all contractual obligations and deliver what has been promised within the agreed scope.

- **Professional Conduct with Suppliers and Contractors:** Maintain fairness when working with vendors and contractors. Avoid unethical kickbacks or undisclosed commissions.

- **Sustainability and Responsibility:** Make environmentally responsible choices and educate clients about sustainable materials and practices.

- **Avoid Plagiarism:** Respect other designers' work and intellectual property. Copying or replicating another designer's work without permission is unethical.

Key Point: Following a strong code of ethics ensures credibility, legal compliance, and a positive reputation in the interior design industry. By adhering to ethical principles, designers create trust-based relationships and maintain industry integrity.

14.2

Maintaining Transparency with Clients

Transparency is key to building a successful and long-lasting client relationship in interior design. Clients invest significant resources into projects, and any ambiguity in pricing, contracts, or project timelines can lead to dissatisfaction or disputes. A transparent approach eliminates confusion, builds trust, and sets clear expectations from the beginning.

How to Ensure Transparency in Design Projects:

- **Provide Detailed Contracts:** Clearly define project scope, deliverables, payment terms, and timelines in a written contract to avoid misunderstandings.

- **Provide Material and Product Specifications:** Share detailed information about the quality, brand, and specifications of materials, finishes, and furnishings being used.

- **Break Down Cost Estimates:** Offer itemized cost estimates, distinguishing between material costs, labor, taxes, and designer fees to give clients a clear understanding of expenses.

- **Clarify Changes and Additional Costs:** If project modifications arise, communicate their cost implications before implementing them. Always document client approvals.

- **Use Open Communication Channels:** Regularly update clients on project progress through meetings, reports, or emails, ensuring they are aware of any developments.

- **Avoid Hidden Commissions:** Be honest about vendor partnerships and disclose any commissions or incentives received for product recommendations.

- **Set Realistic Timelines:** Avoid overpromising and under delivering. Provide practical timeframes for project completion, considering potential delays in material supply or labor.

- **Provide Warranty and After-Sales Support Details:** Clearly explain warranty terms on products and services to prevent future disputes.

Key Point: A transparent approach in pricing, contracts, and project execution minimizes conflicts and strengthens client trust. Open communication fosters a positive design experience and reduces the risk of dissatisfaction.

14.3

Confidentiality and Intellectual Property

Interior designers work with highly personal client information, proprietary design concepts, and confidential project details. Protecting this information is not only a professional obligation but also a key ethical responsibility. Mishandling confidential data or misusing intellectual property can lead to legal issues and reputational damage.

Best Practices for Client Confidentiality:

- **Secure Client Information:** Store client details, design plans, and project documents securely and limit access only to relevant team members.

- **Obtain Permission for Public Use:** Always seek written approval before using project images, designs, or client testimonials for marketing or portfolio purposes.

- **Non-Disclosure Agreements (NDAs):** For high-value projects, signing an NDA can protect both the designer and client from unauthorized sharing of project details.

- **Respect Client Privacy:** Do not discuss project details with third parties without the client's consent, especially in cases where personal preferences or financial details are involved.

- **Handle Design Concepts Responsibly:** Do not share custom design concepts or mood boards with potential clients before formal engagement, as they may use them without hiring you.

Protecting Intellectual Property as a Designer

- **Copyright Your Designs:** For original design concepts, consider registering copyrights to prevent unauthorized duplication.

- **Use Contracts to Define Ownership Rights:** Specify in contracts whether design concepts, drawings, or 3D models remain the property of the designer or are transferred to the client.

- **Be Cautious with Online Sharing:** If posting work on social media or design platforms, watermark your images and ensure proper credit is given.

- **Monitor Industry Trends for Infringements:** Regularly check for unauthorized use of your work and take legal action if necessary.

Key Point: A transparent approach in pricing, contracts, and project execution minimizes conflicts and strengthens client trust. Open communication fosters a positive design experience and reduces the risk of dissatisfaction.

Conclusion

Upholding ethics and professionalism in interior design is essential for long-term success and industry credibility. Adhering to a strong code of ethics, maintaining transparency with clients, and protecting confidentiality and intellectual property create a trustworthy and legally secure practice. By prioritizing these principles, designers not only foster strong client relationships but also contribute to a more responsible and respected interior design industry. Ethical designers stand out in the competitive market, earning client loyalty and setting new benchmarks for professionalism.

Summary & Takeaways

As we reach the final pages of this book, take a moment to reflect on the journey we've been on together. This book was never just about selling—it was about **transforming the way you communicate, present yourself, and build trust with clients.**

Interior design is a field driven by creativity, passion, and an innate ability to transform spaces. But for many designers, the business and sales side often feels like an afterthought or even a challenge.

That's why this book was written—to **bridge the gap between creativity and commerce**, helping designers like you not just survive but thrive in a competitive market.

Sales isn't about manipulation or hard-selling. It's about **understanding people, identifying their needs, and guiding them toward the right solutions.** When done right, selling is an extension of great design—it's about creating an experience that your clients will appreciate, value, and happily invest in.

If you've absorbed even a fraction of the strategies shared in this book and start applying them, you will **immediately notice a difference in your confidence, client interactions, and overall success.** So before we wrap up, let's go over some of the most important lessons once again. This chapter presents the key takeaways from the book, offering a concise summary of the most valuable insights and lessons every reader can apply.

Top 10 Key Takeaways from This Book

Here are the Top 10 Key Takeaways from this book—insights designed to help interior designers confidently navigate the world of sales and turn conversations into conversions

1. Sales is Not Selling—It's Consulting

Clients don't want to feel like they're being "sold" to. They want a trusted guide who helps them make informed decisions. When you shift your mindset from a salesperson to a consultant, your entire approach changes, and clients feel more comfortable investing in your expertise.

2. People Buy Emotionally, Justify Logically

Design is deeply personal, and decisions are often driven by emotions. A client may say they want a "modern kitchen," but what they really want is a space where their family can bond. Tap into those emotions and show how your design can fulfill their deeper needs.

3. Listen More Than You Talk

The most successful designers listen 70% of the time and talk only 30%. Clients will often tell you exactly what they want if you ask the right questions and actively listen. Instead of pitching your ideas immediately, understand their needs first.

4. Value Over Price—Always!

If clients object to your pricing, it means they don't yet see the value in your work. Instead of defending your price, showcase the unique benefits of your design, your expertise, and how your service will save them time, stress, and money in the long run.

5. Master the Art of Storytelling

Facts tell, but stories sell. Instead of just showing your portfolio, tell stories about past clients—how they struggled, what solutions you provided, and how it transformed their lives. A well-told story makes your services memorable.

6. Handling Objections is a Skill, Not a Battle

Objections about price, time, or style are not rejections—they're invitations to provide more clarity. Instead of reacting defensively, ask open-ended questions to uncover the real concern and address it in a way that reassures the client.

7. The Power of "What If We..."

When facing disagreements or client doubts, avoid saying "no" outright. Instead, reframe your response with collaboration:

Instead of: "That's not possible."

Say: "What if we adjusted the design slightly to accommodate that within the budget?"

8. Your Body Language and Tone Matter More Than Words

Studies show that 93% of communication is non-verbal. The way you present yourself—your posture, expressions, and voice—affects how confident and trustworthy you appear. Always maintain a calm, professional, and enthusiastic tone when discussing projects.

9. Follow-Up is the Secret Weapon of Top Designers

Many designers lose projects simply because they don't follow up. Clients are busy, and hesitation is natural. A well-timed follow-up call or message can be the difference between winning or losing a project.

10. Build a Personal Brand and Be Accessible

In today's digital world, clients don't just buy designs—they buy you. Maintain a professional social media presence, share your design journey, and establish yourself as a thought leader. The more visible and approachable you are, the more trust you build.

Glossary

Active Listening: A communication technique used in client meetings where the designer fully concentrates, understands, responds, and remembers what the client is saying. Critical for understanding client needs and building trust.

Aesthetic Preferences: The visual styles and themes a client prefers, such as modern, minimalist, rustic, or industrial, which influence design choices.

As-Built Drawings: Finalized drawings that reflect the actual dimensions and details of a project after construction is completed, often differing from initial blueprints due to changes during construction.

Biophilic Design: A design trend that integrates natural elements (like plants, water, and natural light) into spaces to promote health, wellness, and connection to nature.

Budget-Friendly Solutions: Design options that are cost-effective and allow clients to achieve their desired look without exceeding their financial constraints.

Building Information Modeling (BIM): Advanced software used in architecture and interior design to create detailed 3D models that include the structural, mechanical, and electrical aspects of a project.

Client Persona: A semi-fictional profile representing the ideal client, based on demographics, psychographics, and lifestyle preferences, used to tailor marketing and design solutions.

Code of Ethics: A set of professional principles that interior designers follow to ensure integrity, transparency, and fairness in their work and client relationships.

Concept Design: The early phase of a design project where initial ideas, themes, and visual styles are developed and presented to the client for approval.

Cost-Benefit Analysis: A method of comparing the costs of specific design features with the benefits they offer, used to help clients understand the value of their investment.

Custom-Built: Furniture or design elements made specifically for a project, based on the client's specifications, often involving higher costs and longer lead times.

Design Brief: A document that outlines the client's needs, preferences, budget, and project scope, serving as a reference throughout the design process to ensure alignment between the designer and the client.

Design Fees: The professional charges interior designers levy for their expertise, creativity, and time spent on planning and executing a project.

Design Presentation: A formal presentation where the designer showcases the proposed design concept, including visuals such as 3D renderings, mood boards, and material samples, to help the client visualize the final product.

Demographics: Statistical data related to the client's age, income, family size, and other characteristics that influence design decisions and sales strategies.

Discount: A price reduction offered to clients as an incentive, often used during negotiations to close a deal while protecting profitability.

Empathy: The ability to understand and share the feelings of the client, which helps designers anticipate client needs and alleviate concerns during the sales and design process.

Engineered Materials: Man-made materials, like engineered wood or quartz, designed to offer improved durability, consistency, or cost-effectiveness compared to natural alternatives.

Final Walkthrough: The final inspection of a completed project by the client and designer to ensure everything meets the agreed-upon specifications before handover.

Functionality: The practical and operational aspects of a design, ensuring that spaces are not only aesthetically pleasing but also meet the client's practical needs.

GST (Goods and Services Tax): A government-mandated indirect tax applied to the sale of goods and services, impacting the final cost paid by clients.

Handover: The final step in the design process where the completed project is officially delivered to the client, along with any necessary documentation like warranties, maintenance plans, and as-built drawings.

Interior Design Trends: Popular styles, themes, and design elements that are currently influencing the market, such as minimalism, biophilic design, or sustainable materials.

Installers: Skilled laborers responsible for putting up key elements in a design project, such as furniture, cabinetry, lighting, or flooring.

Lead Generation: The process of attracting and identifying potential clients who are interested in interior design services, often through marketing, referrals, or social media.

Luxury Clients: Clients who typically prioritize high-end materials, custom designs, and exclusive design elements, often with larger budgets and more personalized services.

Margin: The percentage of profit earned on a project after covering material, labor, and overhead costs, ensuring financial sustainability.

Material Selection: The process of choosing specific materials (e.g., flooring, countertops, fabrics) based on the client's aesthetic preferences, functional needs, and budget.

Milestones: Key points in a project's timeline where specific tasks or phases should be completed, such as finalizing design concepts or completing construction phases.

Modular Furniture: Furniture that can be easily configured or adapted to fit different spaces and uses, often used in small or multifunctional areas to maximize space.

Mood Board: A visual presentation of design concepts, including colors, textures, materials, and inspirations, used to communicate the overall aesthetic and feel of a project.

Needs Assessment: The process of determining the client's practical requirements for a space, such as storage needs, layout preferences, or accessibility features.

Negotiation: A strategic discussion between a designer and a client to agree on project pricing, scope, and terms while maintaining value and fairness.

Parametric Design: A method of design using algorithmic thinking, where design elements are generated by changing specific parameters in the software to explore multiple possibilities.

Punch List: A list of minor tasks or corrections that need to be addressed before the final handover of a project, typically identified during the final walkthrough.

Profit: The financial gain remaining after deducting all costs and expenses from the total revenue of a project or business.

Psychographics: Characteristics related to the client's lifestyle, values, and personality, which influence their design preferences and purchasing behavior.

Renderings: Visual representations of a design concept, typically in 3D, used to help clients visualize the final product and make informed decisions about the design.

Referral Program: A system where satisfied clients are incentivized to recommend the designer's services to others, often in exchange for a discount or gift.

Scope: The defined extent of work, deliverables, and responsibilities in an interior design project, outlining what is included and excluded to manage client expectations and project execution.

Scope Creep: The expansion of a project's scope beyond the original plan, often without a corresponding increase in budget or timeline, which can cause delays and additional costs.

Solution Selling: A sales approach that focuses on presenting design concepts as solutions to the client's specific problems, needs, or lifestyle improvements, rather than just as aesthetic choices.

Space Constraints: Limitations related to the size or shape of a room, which affect how furniture, fixtures, and design elements can be arranged.

Sustainable Design: Designing spaces using materials and methods that minimize environmental impact, often through the use of eco-friendly materials, energy-efficient appliances, and waste reduction strategies.

Timeline Management: The process of scheduling and overseeing the timing of each phase in a design project to ensure that everything is completed on schedule.

Value Engineering: The process of optimizing the cost of a project by substituting materials or design elements with more cost-effective alternatives without sacrificing quality or design integrity.

Visual Aids: Tools such as mood boards, 3D renderings, and material samples used during presentations to help clients understand the proposed design.

Warranty: A guarantee provided for materials or workmanship in a project, ensuring that any defects or issues that arise within a specified time frame will be corrected at no cost to the client.

References

REFERENCE

Here's a list of references that informed various sections of the book, covering design trends, sales techniques, project management, and industry practices:

Paul Smith, Sell with a Story: How to Capture Attention, Build Trust, and Close the Sale (2016) – Key strategies for storytelling in sales, applicable to building trust in interior design sales.

Michael W. McLaughlin, Winning the Professional Services Sale (2009): A resource on selling professional services by focusing on consultancy, applicable to designers positioning themselves as trusted advisors.

Christine M. Piotrowski, Designing Commercial Interiors (2016) : An essential reference for commercial interior design, offering insights into the commercial sales process and client engagement.

Mary V. Knackstedt, The Interior Design Business Handbook: A Complete Guide to Profitability (2012) – Practical advice on managing an interior design business, including sales, contracts, and pricing strategies.

Brian Tracy, The Psychology of Selling: Increase Your Sales Faster and Easier Than You Ever Thought Possible (2006) – Provides fundamental sales techniques and understanding client psychology, crucial for handling objections and closing sales in interior design.

Houzz Pro – Industry platform offering marketing and client management tools for interior designers, widely referenced for its sales, marketing, and project management integration.

Architectural Digest – International and Indian editions provide insights into design trends, materials, and global practices, frequently referenced for up-to-date design inspiration and best practices.

NeoCon – Annual design event focused on commercial design, referenced for trends in commercial interiors, materials, and sustainable practices.

India Design ID – India's premier design event, which showcases local and global interior design trends and innovations. Referenced for local trends in Indian interiors and networking opportunities.

Salone del Mobile, Milan – One of the most significant international furniture and design fairs, referenced for the latest global design trends and technological innovations in furniture and interiors.

Revit BIM Software – Building Information Modeling tool used globally by architects and designers, referenced for its relevance in project management, large-scale design, and integration in construction.

Skillshare & Coursera – Platforms offering specialized online courses in interior design, software, and sales techniques. Referenced for continuous learning recommendations and upskilling resources.

Livspace – India's leading interior design and renovation platform, referenced for practical insights on managing large-scale residential projects, client communication, and modern trends in Indian interior design.

Better Interiors – An Indian magazine focused on design trends, materials, and technology, referenced for local industry trends and best practices in Indian interior design.

GoodHomes India – Indian design magazine, referenced for residential interior design trends, including sustainable practices and modular design innovations.

Inside Outside Magazine – Indian publication that focuses on architecture, interiors, and design trends. Referenced for staying updated on innovations and design practices relevant to Indian interiors.

Procore Project Management Software – Widely used in construction and interior design, referenced for managing timelines, budgets, and communication on complex design projects.

Trello – Project management tool for smaller projects, used for tracking tasks, client communications, and team collaboration in design workflows.

V-Ray Rendering Software – Referenced for photorealistic rendering in client presentations and design visualizations, aiding the communication of design concepts.

Architectural Digest India – Referenced for insights into Indian luxury interiors, modular design, and the impact of global trends on local design practices.

Modular Kitchen Planning & Designing Guide by Gopal Dwivedi – A specialized guide offering in-depth knowledge on modular kitchen layouts, material selection, ergonomics, and modern design trends to create efficient and stylish kitchen spaces.

Recommended Books Interior Design Sales:

Title	Description	Why It's Recommended
Sell with a Story by Paul Smith	A guide on using storytelling to sell effectively by building trust and emotionally connecting with clients.	Helps designers use narrative techniques to communicate their design concepts and value, fostering stronger client relationships.
Winning the Professional Services Sale by Michael W. McLaughlin	Focuses on selling professional services, by positioning yourself as a trusted advisor rather than a salesperson.	Excellent for designers looking to improve client engagement and conversion by emphasizing expertise and consultancy.
Designing Commercial Interiors by Christine M. Piotrowski	Provides an overview of the principles of interior design with a commercial focus, including insights on selling in commercial settings.	Useful for understanding the commercial sales process and tailoring solutions to client needs in business environments.
The Interior Design Business Handbook by Mary V. Knackstedt	A practical guide for running an interior design business, including pricing strategies, contracts, and client communication.	Offers detailed insights into managing the business side of design, including how to effectively pitch and sell your services to potential clients.
The Psychology of Selling by Brian Tracy	Covers fundamental techniques on how to understand client psychology and improve sales.	Great for developing sales strategies based on understanding clients' decision-making processes and motivations.
Modular Kitchen Planning and Designing Guide by Gopal Dwivedi	A detailed guide on designing and planning modular kitchens.	The only comprehensive guide in India for learning end-to-end modular kitchen design and planning.
Modular Wardrobe Planning and Designing Guide by Gopal Dwivedi	A detailed guide on designing and planning modular wardrobes.	The only comprehensive guide in India for learning end-to-end modular kitchen design and planning.

About The Author

About The Author / Scan QR Code

Gopal Dwivedi is a distinguished leader in the interior design industry with over 21 years of experience, specializing in modular kitchens, wardrobes, and home interiors. As the **Chief Design Officer** at Livspace.com, India's largest interior design platform, Gopal has played a pivotal role in revolutionizing home design experiences for countless clients. His expertise spans across business strategy, design development, and customer engagement, making him a thought leader in the industry. He has been honored with prestigious awards such as the **Kitchen Professional of the Year** (2014 & 2019) and the Golden Award for Innovative Design of the Year (2023) by ACETECH Bengaluru.

Gopal's passion for empowering interior designers inspired him to write "The Interior Designer's Sales Blueprint". Drawing from his extensive experience in both design and sales, this book offers practical strategies for designers to confidently communicate their value, connect with clients, and close deals effectively. Inspired by his wife Priyanka's journey from designer to accomplished sales expert, Gopal aims to help designers master sales without enduring a long learning curve. His book serves as a comprehensive guide to transforming creative talent into business success, ensuring designers thrive in an increasingly competitive industry.